Brand Stretch

Brand Stretch

**Why 1 in 2 extensions fail
and how to beat the odds**

A brandgym workout

By David Taylor

John Wiley & Sons, Ltd

Other Wiley Editorial Offices

John Wiley & Sons Inc., 111 River Street, Hoboken, NJ 07030, USA

Jossey-Bass, 989 Market Street, San Francisco, CA 94103-1741, USA

Wiley-VCH Verlag GmbH, Boschstr. 12, D-69469 Weinheim, Germany

John Wiley & Sons Australia Ltd, 33 Park Road, Milton, Queensland 4064, Australia

John Wiley & Sons (Asia) Pte Ltd, 2 Clementi Loop #02-01, Jin Xing Distripark, Singapore 129809

John Wiley & Sons Canada Ltd, 22 Worcester Road, Etobicoke, Ontario, Canada M9W 1L1

Wiley also publishes its books in a variety of electronic formats. Some content that appears
in print may not be available in electronic books.

Library of Congress Cataloging-in-Publication Data

Taylor, David, 1964-
   The brand stretch / by David Taylor.
      p. cm.
Includes bibliographical references and index.
  ISBN 0-470-86211-4 (Cloth : alk. paper)
 1. Brand name products--Management. 2. Brand name
products--Marketing. 3. Brand name products--Valuation--Management. 4.
Product management. I. Title.
HD69.B7 T393 2004
658.8′27--dc22

                       2003025486

British Library Cataloguing in Publication Data

A catalogue record for this book is available from the British Library

ISBN 0-470-86211-4

Typeset in 12/15pt Garamond by Laserwords Private Limited, Chennai, India
Printed and bound in Great Britain by Biddles Ltd, Guildford and King's Lynn
This book is printed on acid-free paper responsibly manufactured from sustainable forestry
in which at least two trees are planted for each one used for paper production.

For Anne-Marie

Contents

Preface

Brand stretch is a red-hot topic for businesses around the world and in every sector. After spending billions of dollars on creating, building and defending strong brands, it's payback time. These brands need to give birth to some beautiful and profitable offspring.

Brand stretch has become so important that it is now an issue for the boardroom, not merely the brand team, as Paul Walsh, CEO of global drinks giant Diageo, will testify. Last year's flop of the company's Captain Morgan Gold ready-to-drink extension was headline news in the business press. The resulting $28 million write-down was associated with a drop in the company's share price. In contrast, Procter & Gamble's successful brand extensions, such as Crest SpinBrush and Whitestrips, drove double-digit profit growth and a 14 per cent share price increase. The company's CEO Alan Lafley explained:

> We had a mind-set where innovation had to flow into new categories and new brands exclusively, and all I did was open people's minds to the possibility it could also flow through our established brands (1).

Unfortunately, the odds are that you will be weeping with Walsh rather than laughing with Lafley. Half of all brand stretch launches join Captain Morgan Gold in the overcrowded extension graveyard. One solution is to follow the advice of management guru Jack Trout. He urges you to kick the stretching habit altogether, vehemently defending the old adage of 'one idea, one brand'. However, this means missing out on the huge potential of well-executed brand stretch to create profitable growth. It also flies in the face of today's focus on building fewer, bigger brands, which is driven by pressures such as rising media costs and the need for bargaining power with major retailers (see Figure 1). For example, Unilever has committed to cut its 1600 brands down to 400, with a focus on 40 'star' brands. These remaining brands have to work much harder to deliver growth, with brand stretch one of the key levers to pull. So the real challenge today is not *if* to stretch, but *how* to stretch. The objective of this book is to provide practical help on both the method and mindset needed to boost your chances of winning.

We start by considering the fundamental reason for the appalling success rate of extensions: '*brand ego tripping*'. This causes companies to launch extensions that meet their internal needs, rather than delivering superior value for the consumer. We see how the most celebrated stretching story, *Virgin*, is in fact the biggest brand ego trip ever. An approach called 'brand

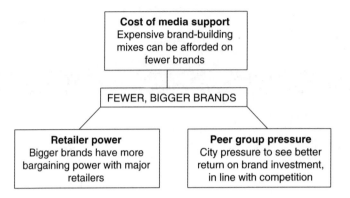

Figure 1: Forces driving fewer, bigger brands.

added value' is then proposed to help you refocus on delivering compelling and competitive consumer benefits. This is illustrated by *Dove's* sequential and successful extension across the 'stretch spectrum'.

The Brand Stretch workout then proposes six practical steps to help you apply the principles of brand added value to boost your chances of success (see Figure 2).

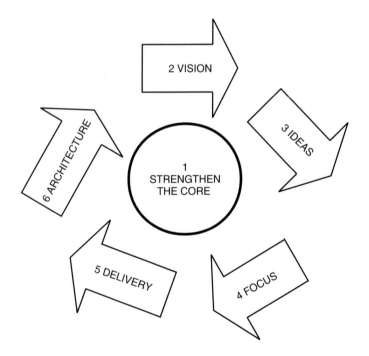

Figure 2: The Brand Stretch workout.

Step One: Strengthen the core emphasizes the importance of a strong core brand and product for successful stretching, illustrated by *Bud Light* in the USA. The risks to the core business from extension are also illustrated, by looking at the decline of the *Tango* brand in the UK soft drinks market.

Step two: Vision looks at developing a clear, ambitious and future-focused vision for your brand. This should help not merely in screening out inappropriate extensions, but also in guiding and inspiring innovation, as illustrated by the repositioning and stretching of *Pampers*.

Step three: Ideas provides practical tips and tricks to help generate ideas for both core range extension and bigger stretching. We look at how mapping the market and understanding consumer needs can uncover opportunities. We also go beyond the consumer to use innovation shortcuts such as your own company and other categories. The *Starbucks Frappuccino* story then illustrates the real challenges of developing extensions, in contrast to the fairytale world of innovation portrayed in most textbooks.

Step four: Focus helps you make the hard calls on which extension ideas to progress and which to kill. Doing fewer, better and bigger extensions is perhaps *the* key factor that will help you boost the chances of success. We see how *easyGroup's* failure to focus on extensions that leverage its core competences has produced enough red ink to sink one of Stelios's supertankers (the chairman's first business).

Step five: Delivery emphasizes the need for extensions to deliver against their promises. The *Apple iPod* story dramatizes the brand and business benefits of excellent execution. New research shows how failing to do this leads to unsuccessful extensions, but also damage to the core brand.

Step six: Architecture proposes a simple and business-focused approach to brand architecture, an area that to date has been overrun with a jungle of jargon. The *Lego* story shows how structuring and organizing the brand's extended offer can aid consumer choice and help align the company's resources.

Like any book, *Brand Stretch* won't transform the fortunes of your brand or business. That requires talent, energy and a decent dose of good luck. However, if the ideas are applied with commitment and conviction, I am confident that it will improve your chances of successful brand extension. After all, with a hit rate as low as 50 per cent, hopefully 'the only way is up'!

Acknowledgements

Only a week after the birth of my first book, *The Brand Gym: A Practical Workout for Boosting Brand and Business*, I went and got pregnant again. Claire Plimmer at John Wiley was good enough to give me a contract for a second book, this time on brand stretch. Little did I know that things would not be easier second time around, as I had expected, but in fact much harder, especially as I now had a growing consulting business to manage at the same time. So the first and biggest vote of thanks goes to my wife Anne-Marie for suffering six months when I worked harder and longer than at any time I can remember. She had to put up with my early alarm calls, late night scribing and many dinners spent sharing my latest ideas, hopes and fears about the book. And Jessica, I promise that from now on the only use of the computer at the weekend will be to play your Snow White CD-ROM.

David Nichols, my good friend and the managing partner of Added Value UK, ripped into the first draft of the book with his usual gusto and gave me the no-holds-barred feedback I needed. This early version went in the bin and I started again, using the new structure he helped me design. Thanks also to Mile Elms of the Marketing Society, who invited me to do a breakfast briefing on 'stretching your brand muscles'. I was able to test out the new concepts with a live audience and see which were hot and which were not. The central theme of brand ego tripping came out of this session. Sarah Holland of Life Support had the monster job of getting signed permission forms for all the images that bring the ideas in the book to life.

Last but most importantly of all, I need to acknowledge the many brand managers and marketing directors who gave up their time to share their experiences with me and help develop the conceptual frameworks. Special thanks go to all the people with whom I have done consulting projects over the last few years (Lever Fabergé, Unilever Bestfoods, Danone, Cadbury Schweppes, SABMiller, Blockbuster and Disney). It is through helping you on the front line of brand building that I really learnt about what works and what doesn't.

Brand stretch – or brand ego trip?

CHAPTER 1

 Headlines

Most companies have caught the brand stretching bug, seeing it as a cheaper and less risky way of launching innovation than creating new brands. In reality the benefits are less cut and dried, with the majority of extensions dying an early death. This poor performance is caused by 'brand ego tripping': an inward focus on the needs of the business, rather than an outward focus on the consumer and competition. This leads to misplaced complacency about a brand's ability to stretch profitably into new areas. To avoid falling into the same trap, you need a ruthless focus on adding value for consumers.

Extension advantages

Over 80 per cent of marketing directors in a recent brandgym survey said that brand extension would be the main way of launching new innovation in the next two to three years (Figure 1.1). They look enviously at the stunning success of extensions such as Bacardi Breezer (a rum-based 'ready-to-drink' product; Figure 1.2) and think 'I'll have some of what they're having!' On paper, the advantages of stretching a brand rather than creating a new one do indeed seem compelling:

- *Consumer knowledge*: using an existing, strong brand to promote a new product or service means that there is less need to create awareness and imagery. Associations have already been established and the main task is communicating the specific benefits of the new innovation. In contrast, a new brand starts from scratch: it has to spend heavily just to get itself known.
- *Consumer trust*: beyond merely being known, strong brands are trusted by consumers to deliver against a particular promise. Done well, an extension uses this reputation to create a compelling value proposition in a new segment or market. A survey by the brandgym

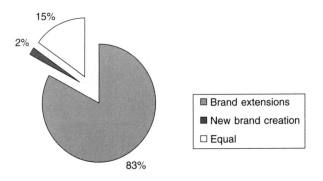

Figure 1.1: Planned use of extensions versus new brands.

Source: the brandgym 2003.

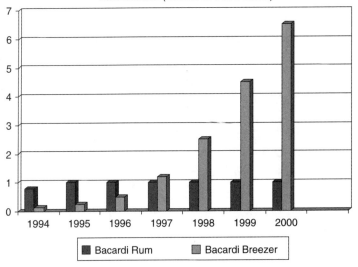

Figure 1.2: Bacardi Breezer sales impact.

showed that 58 per cent of UK consumers would be more likely to try a new product from a brand they knew, versus only 3 per cent for a new brand.

• *Lower cost*: the extension advantages of awareness and reputation mean that you do tend to get 'more bang for your buck' compared to new brands. Studies show that cost per unit of trial is 36 per cent lower and that repurchase is also higher (1). (See Table 1.1.)

Table 1.1: Success rates for extensions versus new brands.

	Trial (index)	Cost per unit of trial (index)	Repeat/loyalty (index)
New brands	100	100	100
Extensions	123	64	161

So why does the success rate suck?

Extensions might be less risky than launching totally new brands. However, the odds are still bad, with only 50 per cent surviving after three years (2). In other words, you are just as well off gambling the company's money on black at the roulette table. But given all that extensions have going for them, why do half end up in the branding graveyard?

The key reason for this appalling performance is *'brand ego tripping'*: being too big for your brand boots and underestimating the challenge of creating a truly compelling and credible extension. As Al Ries aptly put it:

> Companies fall in love with themselves and constantly look for ways to take advantage of their presumably all-powerful brand names (3).

Brand ego tripping leads companies to lose sight of what made them famous in the first place, what helped them deliver differentiation, relevance and value. They end up focusing internally on the needs of the business and its management rather than externally on the needs of the consumer.

Perhaps the biggest and best example of this malaise is Richard Branson's brand ego trip at Virgin. While it is portrayed in many textbooks as *the* example of brand stretching, dig a little deeper and you find another side to the story.

Virgin: The biggest ever brand ego trip?

Taken as a whole, Virgin is a success both in sales and imagery terms. Total group turnover is over $5 billion and the brand is rated as Britain's third most admired, behind Marks & Spencer and Tesco (4). The brand has become a disparate and sprawling mass of more than 25 companies selling everything from lingerie to life insurance. Some of these extensions are shining stars, although there are just as many howling dogs. To understand the reasons for this we need to look at what made Virgin famous in the first place and then see how the company all too often forgot this when extending.

Two sides of the core

For the first 20 of its 30 years, Virgin focused on building two businesses that created the core of the brand. One half of this core is the brand's birthplace of music, with the first Virgin record store being opened on London's Oxford Street in 1971. The company subsequently extended into an area with a direct link to this business by creating a record label in 1973. The first of many PR coups was hiring the then unknown Mike Oldfield, whose *Tubular Bells* album went on to become one of the biggest sellers of all time. These roots in the music business are where the brand acquires its youthful, fun-loving and slightly 'rock 'n roll' personality traits.

The second part of the core is the Virgin Atlantic airline, which alone now accounts for about 40 per cent of the brand's turnover. The launch of Virgin Atlantic in 1984 gave an

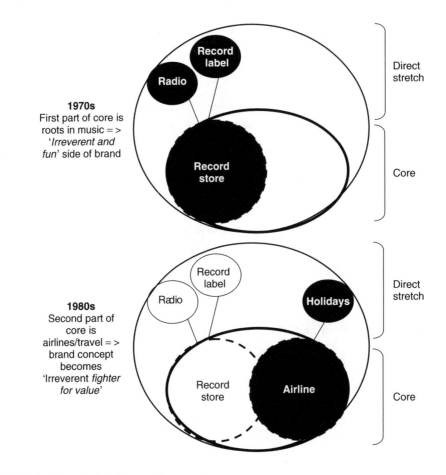

Figure 1.3: Virgin's stretch from a two-part core.

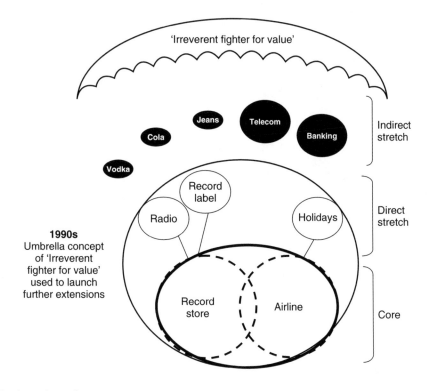

Figure 1.3: (*continued*)

important second set of values: that of a challenger brand fighting for superior value against the big boys like BA. Direct stretching added Virgin Holidays in 1985.

By the end of the 1980s, the Virgin brand was no longer an entertainment business or a pioneering and challenging airline business, but somehow a mix of the two. One way of trying to sum this up is the idea of Virgin being an 'irreverent, fun-loving fighter for value'. The 1990s saw the launch of Virgin's many extensions, which we have now come to associate with the brand (Figure 1.3).

Hits *and* misses

Many branding experts describe Virgin as a 'philosophy' or 'lifestyle' brand that can stretch into pretty much anything, unbound by banalities such as functional product performance. The following quote from a world-famous brand agency sums up this dodgy logic:

> When you've established a strong brand, you've moved beyond the functional product into a realm of values. It makes sense to try to deliver the same emotional benefits in another market (5).

However, as Professor Mark Ritson of London Business School commented in *Marketing* magazine, 'For every Virgin Atlantic or Virgin Music Group there have been numerous failures such as Virgin Cola.' One key reason for this patchy performance is a misunderstanding about both the type of brand that founder Richard Branson really created and the best way of stretching it.

Umbrella brand, not lifestyle brand

In reality, Virgin is not a lifestyle brand. Simply adding the logo to a product will not make people want to buy it. As with other consumer brands, Virgin lacks the 'badge' values to achieve this. This is the domain of brands such as Gucci, where a highly aspirational and rich brand world ties together, and adds value to, a very wide and functionally unrelated 360° set of extensions.

Virgin extensions have worked well when the brand has translated the umbrella concept of being an 'irreverent, fun, value fighter' into compelling and competitive products and services. Virgin Atlantic's success is not down to people flying on it because they buy into a philosophy, but because it's a very good product at a competitive price. A multitude of features such as on-board massages, free ice creams and high-tech video games deliver relevant differentiation. In contrast, Virgin Vodka crashed and burnt because it lacked any brand added value. Where was the challenge? Where was the irreverent fun? The only thing it had going for it was cheapness, following desperate price cuts. Virgin Vodka is far from being the only failed product extension. Virgin Coke in fact achieved only a 3 per cent share in the UK, despite a price 15–20 per cent below Coke. And have you seen many young hipsters chucking out their Levi's or Diesel jeans in favour of Virgin?

As a general rule, Virgin's Robin Hood-like mission of taking on the over-charging and under-delivering bully boys has worked much better in services. There have been (and remain) many good targets to attack. Beyond airlines, Virgin has made good inroads into the mobile phone market in the UK and USA. Its irreverent personality is a refreshing contrast to the conservative communications of Vodafone, T-Mobile and O$_2$. But this is backed up with real service differentiation such as low-frills phones, web-based ways of buying more airtime and no long-term contracts.

Spotting an ego tripper

There are several key lessons to learn from Virgin's brand ego trip:
- *Neglecting the core*: you have to wonder whether Virgin would have been even bigger and stronger if the company had spent more time on developing and nurturing the core areas

of travel and entertainment. Instead, Virgin actually sold off its record business in 1992 to Thorn EMI to help fund the brand ego trip of the 1990s. To quote Mark Ritson again, 'Only time will tell if Virgin's cash cows can continue to supply the nourishment for its stable of failures.'

- *Forgetting what made you famous*: part of Virgin's success is down to Branson's admirable bravery at taking on the big boys. With airlines and financial services, he rightly spotted competitors that were over-pricing and under-performing and did us all a favour by delivering something better. Emotional values were underpinned by a strong functional point of difference (Figure 1.4). However, with cola, vodka and jeans Virgin failed to develop a product that was faithful to the brand's promise: these extensions were 'all sizzle and no sausage'.

- *Failing to understand consumers and markets*: the lack of real success in jeans, cola and vodka also reflects a failure to understand the needs in these markets. As discussed earlier, consumers mostly want aspirational, fashionable badge values (e.g. Diesel, Armani) and/or strong heritage (e.g. Levi's). Virgin had neither of these and was left with only one option: price cutting. However, even here the brand could not compete effectively, as it lacked the critical mass needed to achieve economies of scale and so drive down prices. Retail competitors such as Wal-Mart/Asda were much better positioned to produce low-cost, me-too vodkas, colas and jeans and still make good profits.

- *Scatter-gun stretching*: this led to a fragmentation of financial and human resources. Selective extension into new areas faithful to the Virgin promise could perhaps have delivered a better return on investment. Branson is of course in a very different position to most people reading this book, in that he has no shareholders to please and lots of his own hard-earned cash to play with.

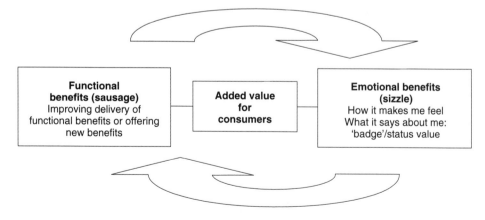

Figure 1.4: Adding value for the consumer.

- *Neglecting execution*: this can lead to poor product performance and even brand damage, as was the case with the mis-selling scandal at Virgin Energy. The door-to-door salespeople employed by venture partner London Electricity hadn't read Virgin's customer service charter. They used dodgy deals and hard selling to flog their wares and watchdog Energywatch received many complaints. Some consumers even had their electricity accounts charged after signing up for information about cheap Virgin CDs and airline tickets!

The bottom line on the Virgin story is the same as that throughout this book. Promise something relevant to the consumer and deliver the goods and you will build both brand and business. Fail to do this and no amount of marketing support or brand philosophy will save your bacon.

Virgin summary
1. Remember what made you famous.
2. Have some sausage not just sizzle.
3. Understand the consumer and the competition.
4. Execution is king.

Shotgun weddings

Another aspect of brand ego tripping is extending for tactical reasons that serve the company's short-term needs, not those of the consumer. These brand/extension relationships are mostly doomed to fail, like a wedding based on the need to save on taxes or secure immigration status. It seems that brand extensions are often not handled with the same strategic rigour and discipline as new brand creation.

Adding novelty

Adding novelty and newness is often put forward as a reason to extend a brand. However, this should be viewed as a potential bonus, not the main rationale. The risk is that it results in gimmicks that simply steal sales from existing users looking for a change. Time will tell if the latest flavour variations of Coke, with lemon and vanilla, have anything more than temporary appeal. In contrast, Coke Light/Diet Coke tapped into a significant consumer need for more healthy products and has gone on to constitute a major proportion of the brand's sales.

Copying the competition

Knee-jerk, me-too reactions to competitive extensions usually deliver disappointing results. The first risk is adding credence and credibility to the new segment and so actually helping the competitive extension. Also, being late to market with a me-too product usually means a smaller share of the new pie. One more cost-effective alternative may be to 'shift weight' with your existing products to claim the new benefit. For example, rather than copying Coke's lemon extension with its own 'Pepsi Twist' product, Pepsi could have ploughed the cash into communicating how great its core product is with a slice of lemon.

If the decision is taken to extend in reaction to a competitive move, the ambition should be to leapfrog the competition with relevant differentiation and a stronger mix. Nurofen launched a painkiller for children in the UK to compete with the leading brand, Calpol. It was able to demonstrate that its Ibuprofen-based formula was longer lasting than Calpol and so helped a sick child get through the night without waking up. Any parent will know how powerful this benefit is!

Winning shelf space

Improved shelf presence through additional listings is another knock-on benefit of launching a new extension, but again should not be the main reason for stretching. While major retailers might be persuaded to list a new extension based on the strength of the brand, they will quickly weed it out if it fails to perform.

Quitting the brand ego trip

Recognizing and rectifying the problems of brand ego tripping can significantly improve your odds of winning the extension game. However, research by the brandgym suggests that many marketers are still blind to the poorness of their extension efforts to date. A sample of marketing directors believed that almost 90 per cent of consumers had become *more* positive about brand stretch over the last 5–10 years. Nevertheless, when a panel of 1000 UK consumers was asked the same question, the results were less definite. Only 29 per cent were positive, with a huge 61 per cent undecided (Figure 1.5). A quick look at the 'extension graveyard' (Figure 1.6) helps explain their scepticism (6).

Brand added value

The key to quitting the brand ego trip is to refocus on 'brand added value'. Importantly, this goes beyond the dominant extension theory of 'brand fit', which suggests that anything fitting the brand's image *today* is a good idea. Brand added value requires the use of brand *vision* to inspire and guide the development of extensions that are genuinely relevant and differentiated.

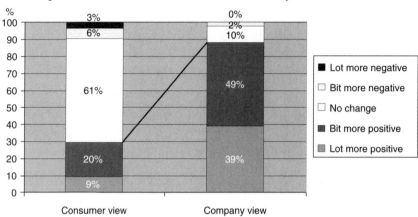

Change in consumer attitudes to brand stretch over last 5–10 years

Figure 1.5: Consumer versus company views on brand stretch.

Source: the brandgym 2003.

Figure 1.6: The extension graveyard.

Table 1.2: The stretch spectrum.

	Core range extension*	Direct stretch*	Indirect stretch*	360° stretch**
Dove	Dove Sensitive bar	Dove shower gel	Dove shampoo	Dove spas
Other examples	Gillette Mach 3 razor BMW 318 Cabriolet	Gillette Series shave gel BMW X5 4 × 4	Gillette deodorant BMW mountain bikes	Gillette sportswear BMW driving holidays
Description	New format or flavour as addition to core product range	Stretch into adjacent markets with a direct link to core range	Stretch to a more distant market with less obvious link to core range	Extremely large range of products with no obvious functional linkage to core
Linkage to the core	Format	Reason to believe and/or complementary usage	Umbrella concept and brand personality	Badge values
In-store position	Directly next to core range	Close to core range, same fixture	Further from core range. Different fixture or even different store	Different stores, or sections of a 'flagship' brand store
Mode of consumption	Similar type of usage to core product, though could be different occasion	Similar type of usage to core product, though could be different occasion	Different to core product	Very varied

Notes: * All real examples
     ** Possible brand ego trips

Dove is one brand that has added real value for consumers as it has extended across the stretch spectrum (Table 1.2).

Dove: Brand added value in action

Brand stretch was a key driver of Dove's explosive growth during the 1990s. Coupled with geographic expansion, it helped grow sales fivefold, to almost $1 billion (Figure 1.7). The brand continues to grow at 20 per cent per year and is well on its way to hitting the $2 billion mark in the next few years.

Strong from the core

The original Dove bar is at the heart of the brand, the purest and most powerful incarnation of the promise to 'not dry skin thanks to its 1/4 moisturizing cream'. In the US home market the brand waited 40 years before its first major extension. Other, newer markets did not wait

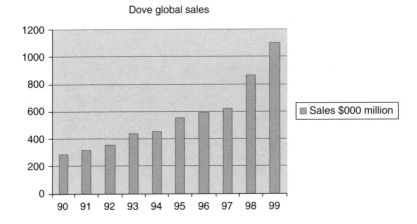

Figure 1.7: Dove sales growth.

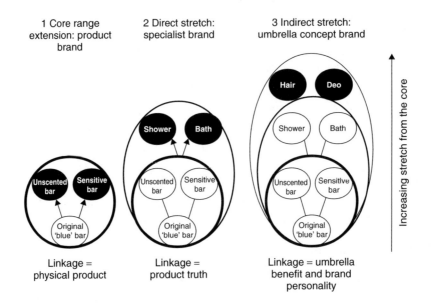

Figure 1.8: Sequential stretching of Dove.

so long. However, careful controls ensured that new extensions were introduced only after two 'traffic lights' had gone green:

- A strong bar business had been built.
- The brand had satisfactory scores on attribute ratings for mildness and moisturization.

Stretching then went through several stages (Figure 1.8).

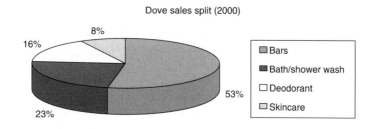

Figure 1.9: Dove sales split.

Stage one: Core range extensions

At this stage, Dove remained a 'product brand' with a single format. Stretching started with core range extensions on the bar by adding new versions, such as one for sensitive skin that now accounts for up to a third of sales. The importance of the core bar business is shown by the fact that it still represents 55 per cent of the brand's sales and an even bigger share of profit (Figure 1.9). Further growth of the bar, through product and pack innovation, remains a key source of profitable growth.

Stage two: Direct stretch

The next stage was direct stretch into adjacent personal wash markets, such as bath and shower products. Here, the brand's mild moisturization benefit provided relevant differentiation, supported by the 1/4 moisturizing cream promise. Dove now had a broader offer than before, but remained a specialist brand focused on personal washing. Selection of extensions was disciplined and based on the brand's added value in two key areas:

- *Strong product delivery*: each new extension was rigorously evaluated and debated to ensure that it lived up to the brand's high product standards. The objective was to be able to make a 'provable promise', by delivering a noticeable improvement in the skin that women could see and feel for themselves.
- *Innovative product and pack forms*: these proved to be key signals of change and differentiation. For example, Dove Ultra Moisturising Body Wash has two differently coloured and visible components (blue mild cleansers and pink moisturizers) that are combined when you squeeze out the product.

Stage three: Indirect stretch

The third and most ambitious part of the stretching programme was to move into more distant markets that did not have a direct link to the personal wash area. Dove became an 'umbrella concept brand' based on the broader idea of 'simple, mild moisturization'. These ideas were hotly debated, as they pushed the brand boundaries further than had been imagined possible by many senior managers. Interestingly, the project champions came not from the brand's US homeland, but from two of the younger Dove markets.

Italy had evidence that consumers were looking for more skin-friendly products in the deodorant category. They saw an opportunity to combine Dove's benefit of skin mildness with Unilever's competence in deodorants. The go-ahead for a trial launch was based on two key factors. First, the sales and profit potential was significant. Second, the Italian business was in good health, with a solid bar and personal wash foundation. The test was a resounding success, with the brand taking a significant share. The product was rolled out across Europe and then into the USA.

The team in Taiwan had an even more radical idea: Dove haircare. They wanted to move Dove beyond gentle cleaning of skin to deliver the same benefit on hair. This move was once more greeted with concern and even outright opposition. Surely this was a stretch too far, even for Dove? A market test was started and proved to be a huge success. Again, the product was rolled out internationally.

Consistency counts

A final lesson from the Dove story is the benefit of consistent marketing. It was one of Unilever's first brands to be managed on a truly global basis, with senior management responsible for the quality of the rollout. The brand has been consistent in its communication campaign, making use of real women telling their stories about Dove. This is a key part of building the brand's approachable, empathetic personality that provides additional 'glue' to tie together the extensions.

Dove summary

1. Build from a strong core.
2. Stretch selectively where the brand adds real value.
3. A strong product truth is a great help in stretching.
4. Consistency counts.

The Brand Stretch workout

The rest of the book will take you through a simple, practical, five-step programme designed to boost your chance of winning the brand extension game. Each of the five steps seeks to address one of the aspects of brand ego tripping that we saw earlier (Table 1.3).

Table 1.3: Brand ego trip problems and solutions.

Workout	Problem	Solution
1 Strengthen the core	Neglecting the core brand/product range	Protect and grow the core
2 Vision	Forgetting what made you famous in the first place	Clear vision to ensure extensions have added value
3 Ideas	Extensions are company not market driven	Use market and consumer insight as a catalyst for ideas
4 Focus	Scatter-gun stretching leads to dwarf extensions	Fewer, bigger ideas that build brand *and* business
5 Delivery	Execution fails to deliver against promises	Excellence in execution as a key source of differentiation
6 Brand architecture	Confusing range for both consumer and company	Structure that aids consumer choice and company efficiency

 ## Key takeouts

1. The success rate of brand extensions is poor.
2. The fundamental problem is the brand ego trip that many marketing teams are on.
3. Companies need to focus their efforts on adding value for consumers, with emotional values underpinned by functional performance.

Checklist 1: Brand Stretch – or brand ego trip?

	Yes	No
• Are your primary reasons for extending consumer and not company centric?	☐	☐
• Do you have ways of delivering functional performance not merely emotional sizzle?	☐	☐
• Do you fully understand and respect the competition in the new area you are stretching into?	☐	☐
• Have you understood and adapted to the rules of the new category?	☐	☐
• Is the importance of excellent execution fully embraced or seen as a 'nice to have'?	☐	☐

 ## Handover

We have seen the theoretical advantages that extensions should have over new brand creation. By leveraging a known and trusted brand, an extension should have a much better chance of success. However, the problem of brand ego tripping means that the harsh reality is an appalling success rate. Focusing on brand added value is the key to boosting your chances of successful stretching. In the next chapter we will look at the first vital step in delivering brand added value: having a strong core brand and product to stretch in the first place.

Step One: Strengthen the core

CHAPTER 2

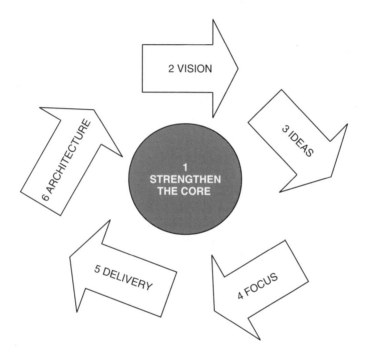

Headlines

The first step for successful stretching is to ensure you have a strong and healthy brand that can add real value to new extensions. If your brand is underperforming it may actually *decrease* the appeal of new products or services, weighing them down with unhelpful baggage. At the heart of most strong brands is a strong core product that defines the brand concept, builds credibility and provides an important source of profit. Therefore, the first priority of extension should be to build and strengthen the core range, before considering stretching further into new areas.

In shape to stretch?

Several studies have confirmed what common sense tells you: extensions of strong brands are more likely to succeed than those of weaker brands (1). As a general manager at Procter & Gamble liked to say, 'It's hard for a sick mother to give birth to a healthy child.' Therefore, the first step in boosting your chances of successful stretching is to ensure that your core brand is strong and healthy.

Starbucks eventually extended its brand into Frappuccino® and DoubleShot™ coffee drinks, sold in supermarkets through a joint venture with the Pepsi-Cola Company. It has also built the number one super premium coffee ice cream in the USA through a partnership with Dreyer's Grand Ice Cream, Inc. (Figure 2.1). However, these new product extensions were only successful because of the strength of the core Starbucks coffee shop business, built up over a period of 10 years.

There are many sophisticated measures of brand health, but at its most basic there are two factors that really count:

- *Sales*: has the brand been growing healthily and consistently over the last few years? Also, is it able to support a price premium or at least parity versus key competitors, or are you having to cut prices to keep up?

Figure 2.1: Starbucks extension that builds off a strong core.

- *Brand image*: does the brand perform strongly on the key dimensions that drive brand choice? If it is performing poorly in its core area of expertise, then the credibility of a new extension is likely to be undermined.

Repositioning to stretch

For a sick brand, or one that has some negative associations, *repositioning* may be needed to get it in shape to stretch. For example, the Lucozade glucose drink was sold for many years as a drink for sick children with the slogan 'Lucozade aids recovery'. It was packaged in big bottles covered in yellow cellophane, had a medicinal image and limited opportunities to stretch. In the 1980s the brand was relaunched with a positive energy promise, using a famous UK athlete called Daley Thompson. The glucose product truth remained the same, but it was used to support a bigger, more everyday concept. Smaller bottles for individual use were launched in smaller stores where younger people bought soft drinks. This relaunch served as a platform for the brand to stretch into the sports drink area with Lucozade Sport in 1991. The brand has built a dominant 70 per cent share of this large and fast-growing market, supported by sponsorship of top UK sports people such as the soccer player Michael Owen (2).

The heart of a healthy brand

Most healthy *brands* have at their heart a strong core *product*. This 'flagship' product best encapsulates the brand concept and is often the original one with which the brand was born. Johnson's now has a broad range (Figure 2.2), yet most US consumers still think of the baby shampoo when asked about the brand (3). Other examples of core products are the Porsche 911, the Timberland boot, Kellogg's Cornflakes and the Lacoste polo shirt. Having a strong core product gives you two key advantages: profits and credibility.

Source of profit

At a most basic level, the core product is often the biggest and most profitable in the range. We saw in the last chapter that even though Dove has stretched into many new areas, the core bar still makes up over half of sales. In addition, core products are often simpler than subsequent extensions and so may have higher gross margins.

Source of credibility

In many cases, the core product is a source of credibility and authenticity. Andy Fennell, Smirnoff's president of global marketing, sees this working for the Smirnoff Ice pre-mixed

Figure 2.2: Johnson's core product and extensions.

drink (Figure 2.3): 'As with any innovation and parent brand, Smirnoff Red vodka brings stature and credibility to its extension' (4). This is an important difference over new brands such as Reef. Smirnoff Ice might be the fastest-growing part of the brand, already selling 4.7 million cases that make up 22 per cent of the brand's volume, but the company still invests heavily in the core vodka. Failure to do so could lead to the erosion of the foundation on which the extension was built. This could undermine the appeal of Smirnoff Ice but also future vodka-based brand extensions.

Credibility
and
authenticity

Figure 2.3: Smirnoff Red vodka as source of credibility for extension.

Reproduced by permission of Diageo.

Anchoring the core range

Extending the core range should be the first priority for brand stretching. This tends to be easier if the range has a clear 'anchor': the simplest, purest and most authentic version. The Magnum bar is the core product at the heart of the brand and within this core the original chocolate version is the anchor. Flavour extensions such as white chocolate or almond can be positioned against this original version. They can focus on emphasizing specific attributes and benefits, rather than communicating the whole product concept (Figure 2.4).

Even though the anchor version often declines as new extensions are launched, smart companies continue to support them. They recognize that these products are an important source of credibility on which the newer products rely. This is why the traditional red and white of Classic Coke is featured in the brand's advertising and soccer World Cup sponsorship. Ferrari Formula 1 cars sport the red of the Marlboro anchor version, not the gold of Marlboro Lights (Table 2.1).

The US beer market shows the advantages of having an anchor version and the drawbacks of not having one.

Anchor version: chocolate   Other flavours: almond and white chocolate

Figure 2.4: Anchor version and additional flavours.

Reproduced by permission of Unilever plc.

Table 2.1: Core products and anchor versions.

Masterbrand	Core product	Anchor version of core product	Other versions
Bacardi	Rum	Carta Blanca	Limon, Bacardi 8 (aged rum)
Kellogg's	Cornflakes	Original	Chocolate, Crunchy Nut
Malboro	Cigarettes	Red top	Light, Medium, Ultra Light
Smirnoff	Vodka	Red (40°)	Black (50°)
Dove	Bar	Original blue	Sensitive skin, Unscented

Bud and Bud Light: Sun and planets

Budweiser the brand has Budweiser the product as its anchor: not Bud Original or Bud Classic, just Bud. This original version has been around since 1879 and the pack identity has stayed consistent over this time. It stars in the brand's famous 'Wassup' and 'Frogs' advertising campaigns and is also used in ongoing product quality communications selling the benefits of fresh beer. Satellite extensions can then orbit around this sun and draw on its authentic imagery.

Bud Light has been a particular success, tapping into the growing US interest in lower-calorie products. It benefits from all the authenticity, heritage and taste credentials of the Bud anchor version, while being free to focus on its specific taste and more irreverent, younger personality. It now accounts for almost half of the brand's sales, a fair part of which has come from the original Bud version. Extension haters such as Jack Trout point their finger at this and protest that 'Bud has too many "Buds for you" and Bud Light is eating into basic Budweiser' (5). However, what he fails to point out is that the brand as a whole has *grown by 40 per cent* since the Bud Light launch.

In contrast, competitor Miller's did not establish a strong anchor version, making extending its core range much harder. The original Miller beer was Miller High Life. However, when Miller launched a revolutionary light beer in 1975, it effectively decided to launch it as a new brand: Lite (from Miller). The Miller brand was subsequently made more prominent on the pack, but the emphasis remained on Lite. While one reason for this strategy was a concern to insulate Miller High Life from any negative publicity about light beer, another issue was that Miller High Life was not a simple anchor version in the same way that Bud was. A further major extension followed in 1985 with Miller Genuine Draft, a more premium, upscale beer. Again, this ended up effectively being a new brand, with 'MGD' becoming the shorthand 'bar call' and being featured on pack. Miller has effectively ended up with three different brands that share the same brewery name. Each has its own distinctive positioning, with the emphasis on Lite, MGD and High Life. There is less synergy between these products than between Bud and Bud Light. This model does seem to have been less successful in driving growth, with total Miller sales lower than when MGD was launched.

Miller tried to rectify the lack of an anchor version, by retro-fitting one. 'Miller beer' was launched in 1996 with $50 million of marketing support and a great-tasting product. However, it suffered from the lack of a clear reason to exist. Why switch from good old Bud to this newly created Miller beer that

> **Bud Light summary**
>
> 1. An anchor version makes the launch of core range extensions easier.
> 2. It is hard to launch an anchor version after the fact.

lacked roots, history and credibility? The launch was a flop and the product was withdrawn. New owner SAB has stabilized brand sales and is working on relaunch plans.

Even a strong core product and anchor version can be undermined by extensions if brand stretching is not properly managed. We will now look at some of the risks for the core range and how to avoid them.

Risky business

While the reaction of the anti-extension pack led by Jack Trout tends to be over the top, they are right to flag up the risks to the core business (Figure 2.5). These include stealing thunder, cannibalization and the new toy syndrome.

Stealing thunder

Extensions can benefit from exciting innovations that would have been better off revitalizing the existing core range. The basic rule is to ask if there is a trade-off involved in the product change.

When more means more

Upgrading the core product is a better route when the product change improves performance with no trade-off. This is how mainstream car makers like Ford responded to the increased demand for safety features such as ABS brakes and air bags pioneered by Volvo. Rather than creating their own safer car extensions, they integrated these features into existing models. This was first done as optional extras, creating incremental revenues. Eventually, these features became expected in a car and were offered as standard.

When more means less

Extension is the best route when modifying the product adds some benefits but risks undermining others. When Head & Shoulders wanted to respond to the trend for more

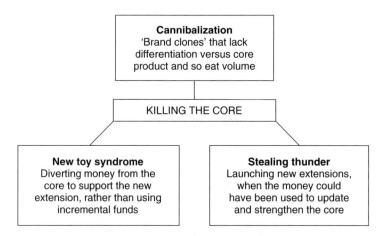

Figure 2.5: Extensions can seriously damage your brand health.

regular hair washing, a frequent-use version was developed. It had a lower amount of active ingredient and a milder cleaning system. If this had been used to replace the original version, existing users may have been disappointed with the lower efficacy and left the brand. The new product was launched as a range extension and succeeded in building sales by about 10 per cent, attracting new users to the brand.

Cannibalization

As the name suggests, this is the risk of an extension eating up other family members. The biggest risk occurs with range extensions that are 'brand clones', lacking differentiation versus the existing products. Crest spent decades launching new toothpaste twists such as tartar control, gum protection and whitening. In the USA, share halved from 50 per cent with one product to 25 per cent with 50 products (6). Each introduction competed for the same usage occasion and introduced novelty value but not enough added value to create incremental growth. What most people wanted was an 'all-in-one' version, which was successfully launched by Colgate as Colgate Total.

Eating profits

Eating volume is bad enough. However, the story gets even worse when extensions cost more owing to extra goodies yet fail to be priced up, resulting in a lower profit margin. So not only does the new eat the old, the profitability of the total business goes south. This problem often happens because the changes made cost the company more without adding relevant benefits for the consumer. If you are really adding value, then you should be able to price up.

Launch and run

The problem of cannibalization is made more likely by the 'revolving door' syndrome on many brand teams, where new people come on board every couple of years. The tendency is to 'launch and run': do an extension that boosts sales in the short term then move on before the cracks in the core product start to show up. The type of sales chart shown in Figure 2.6 is all too common. Note that much of the initial volume lift is 'pipeline' to fill up the shelves of key customers. The ongoing level is often not as high, especially if the repurchase rate is poor. The new brand manager inherits the problem and often makes the same mistake: another extension that further weakens the core, and so on. You end up with the same or fewer sales, spread over more products.

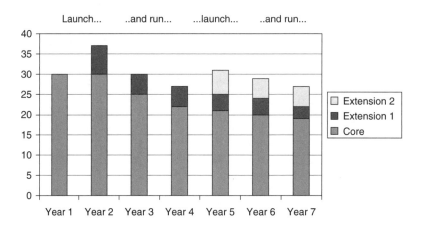

Figure 2.6: Eating your mum and dad.

Some cannibalization of the core will happen with most extensions, but the level can be minimized and need not be life threatening. Launching extensions that add real value is one way of doing this, as discussed earlier. However, perhaps the biggest mistake to avoid is eating into the human and financial resources of the core product.

New toy syndrome

There is always a temptation to spend time, money and energy on the sexy new extension rather than on the core business. This is why funds for a new extension are sometimes taken from the core range's budget, leaving it exposed to competition. In many cases, the return on investment from spending on the new extension is less than if the money had been kept for the bigger core product. For example, one manager enthusiastically told how his brand new extension had added 100 000 extra units of sales. However, he seemed to have overlooked the fact that growing the 4 million units of the core version by 2.5 per cent might have delivered a better return on investment.

Sometimes the new toy syndrome happens when brands stretch into totally new areas and fund this out of the core product range's budget. It is also a risk for mono-product brands, when attention is moved away from an anchor version onto new versions, such as formats or flavours. This was the problem that caused the dramatic decline of one of the UK's once most successful brands, Tango.

Tango: Taking the eye off the orange ball

Tango achieved great success in the UK soft drinks market in the 1990s by dramatizing the refreshing taste hit of its fizzy orange drink in an entertaining and zany way. Big fat orange men, orange gloved hands and bursting orange balloons were all used to show that 'You know when you've been Tango'd'. However, the brand then fragmented its marketing behind a series of new flavour extensions at a time when Coke was single-mindedly pushing Fanta Orange. Tango lost the leadership it had once had, both in terms of sales and brand imagery. As *Marketing* magazine commented, 'Fanta is indeed trouncing Tango, which is now struggling to revive its seriously declining sales' (7). Tango value sales in major multiples nose-dived by 21 per cent in 2002, while Fanta sales were up by 69 per cent (8). The explicit strategy of the giant from Atlanta to 'kill Tango' seems close to becoming true.

Telling too many stories

The big mistake Tango made was not that it launched new flavours such as Apple and Tropical. It was the *way* it launched them that hurt the brand. Each variant got its own advertising campaign, media support, promotion and sales push. Rather than helping build one big brand idea, each version was given its own personality. The brand fragmented its efforts by telling several different stories, rather than several chapters of the *same* story. This required not only money but, just as importantly, management time from the brand team, agency and sales force. As often happens, much of the human and financial resources for the new flavours was diverted from the anchor version. To make matters worse, this happened just as Fanta was launching a full-scale, focused attack to 'own orange'.

Second, Tango's new flavours were less appealing than the original orange, failing to beat or even match the competitive products against which they were targeted. There was a lack of added value and the brand was up against strong competition. Why would a happy Lilt user switch to Tango Tropical when it tasted the same or less good? In addition, the 'refreshment hit' concept worked less well with fruity tropical and cherry than with zingy orange. The extra sales from the new variants failed to compensate for the loss of volume on the anchor orange version.

Further fragmentation

Fragmentation was made worse through a proliferation of sizes and formats and the addition of new diet versions on all but one of the flavours. The result was literally an explosion in the number of different 'stock keeping units' (skus). Not only was the total business smaller than before all the extensions, it was divided up between this multitude of products rather than the original four or five.

Tango did finally get back to basics late in 2002. A new campaign was launched based on the 'hit of the whole fruit', with a single-minded focus on the core orange variant. Even the old tagline of 'You've been Tango'd' was resurrected. The early signs are encouraging, but it may be too little, too late for Tango.

Tango summary

1. Neglect the core at your peril.
2. Avoid stealing from the core to promote new range extensions.
3. Selectively extend the core, ensuring that new products add value versus those of competitors.

Key takeouts

1. Most strong brands have at their heart a strong core product that provides a healthy profit stream and a source of credibility.
2. Core range extension is made easier if there is an anchor version to serve as a reference point.
3. Poor use of brand extension can seriously damage the brand, by stealing volume, diluting profit and diverting investment.

Checklist 2: Strengthen the core

	Yes	No
• Is your brand healthy and strong versus key competition in both image terms and sales growth?	☐	☐
• Do you have a core product along the lines of a Dove bar or a Timberland boot?	☐	☐
• Within this core range, are you clear about the anchor version (sun) against which you can position future extensions (planets)?	☐	☐
• Where you are considering a core range extension, do you *need* to extend rather than upgrading the core product?	☐	☐
• Are you maintaining strong support on the core product to avoid the trap of the 'new toy syndrome'?	☐	☐

Handover

We have now established the importance of having a strong and healthy brand as the first part of a brand stretch programme. In addition, the key roles played by the core product range and anchor version have been reviewed. The next chapter will look at developing a future-focused vision to guide and inspire brand stretching.

Step Two: Vision

CHAPTER 3

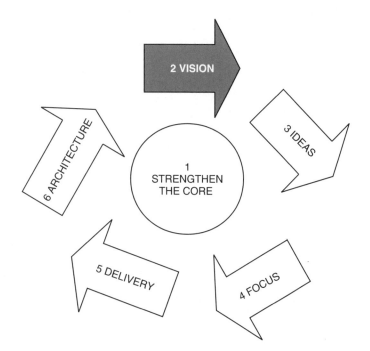

 ## Headlines

With a healthy brand and core product, attention can be turned to the future. Developing a clear and ambitious brand vision is a great stimulus for successful stretch. By encouraging you to develop a broader definition of your market, it helps highlight opportunities for brand stretch and potential threats from competitors. It also gives the whole team a sense of direction, assisting in ensuring that extensions not only build sales, but also play a role in building one big brand idea. Without such a vision, new extensions are free to take on a life of their own, resulting in a lack of brand coherence and a dilution of the core message.

GPS for brands

Stretching a brand without a clear vision is like driving in the dark with no headlights. You have no idea of where you are going, the obstacles to avoid and which routes to take. Sooner rather than later you crash. Disneyland Paris (DLP) experienced this problem in the mid-1990s when developing the launch plan for Space Mountain, a new multimillion-dollar attraction. The dilemma was how heavily to promote this extension, as it was much more grown-up and thrilling than the current attractions. Should such an exciting and almost 'white knuckle' ride take the lion's share of the following year's budget or be launched more quietly? This was a big call to make, as the park had failed to meet its targets, was losing money and according to the press was on the brink of bankruptcy.

Two simple questions related to solving this issue left the Disney team perplexed: 'What is the "masterbrand" positioning, the vision for Disneyland Paris as a whole?' and 'What role could the Space Mountain extension play in bringing this vision to life?' The number of different answers from around the table showed that there was no agreed positioning for anything! The team was driving in the dark.

As a first step, a DLP masterbrand vision was developed by a team from different functions across the park, such as marketing, sales and 'imagineering' (Disney's amazing team of new product developers). The resulting brand promise captured the active, rather than passive, nature of the DLP experience and its appeal to everyone, whatever their age:

> Disneyland Paris is a magical land where people of all ages can live out the adventures they have dreamt of.

With a clearer idea of the masterbrand positioning, it was much easier to assess the potential of the Space Mountain extension. Consumer research confirmed that it did have the excitement and thrill factor that the Disney team had anticipated. Importantly, though, these sensations were an integral part of an amazing, themed adventure. What is more, this adventure, of going from the earth to the moon, was one that everyone had dreamt of. In other words, Space Mountain was a perfect dramatization of the masterbrand positioning. It was agreed that Space Mountain would be the 'star product' for the 1994 relaunch: the 'Levi's 501 of the park'. In consequence, a significant part of the annual budget was put behind the launch. Visitor numbers grew significantly and the park went into profit for the first time, going on to become the biggest tourist attraction in Europe.

This story shows the benefits of a clear and compelling positioning that pins down and substantiates your brand's competitive advantage. It works like a GPS (Global Positioning System), helping you navigate to your desired destination, telling you when you are on track and when to change direction (Figure 3.1). It also helps inspire and guide the generation

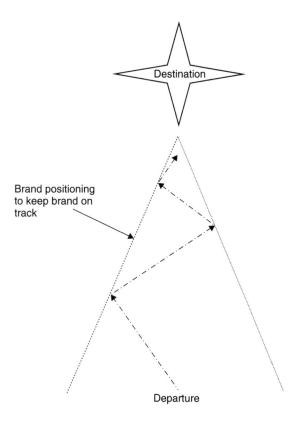

Figure 3.1: GPS for brands.

of relevant and differentiated extension ideas. However, several challenges face any team undertaking this task.

The masterbrand challenges

Positioning a mono-product brand is relatively straightforward, provided that there is a clear product truth on which to build. However, as you start to stretch, the brand positioning challenge becomes a whole lot harder. On the one hand, you need a big idea that makes sense of the wider product range, ensuring that coherence and consistency are maintained. Otherwise, each product takes on a life of its own and the masterbrand is relegated to the role of a token endorser of quality. On the other hand, you need a vision that stimulates rather than stifles innovation.

This task is made all the harder by the numerous stakeholders who want a say in the strategy development process. Cutting them out with a dictatorial approach might work if you are a visionary and all-powerful CEO like Michael Dell or Jeff Bezos, but in most companies this is a recipe for dissent and disaster. However, the alternative of seeking input from different sources presents its own challenges.

Too many cooks spoil the brand

Many companies struggle with masterbrand positioning, as they work 'bottom up', starting with the existing product range and trying to find a common conceptual thread. This is like trying to solve a jigsaw puzzle with too many pieces, and ones not even designed to fit together in the first place. Teams from different product categories or geographic markets invariably end up 'fighting their corner'. A watered-down compromise is drafted to keep everyone happy, but this bland and uninspiring strategy gathers dust in the filing cabinet, being of no practical use to anyone.

Back to the future

A better way to develop a masterbrand positioning is to start with the future and work back to reality. This also involves working 'top down': from masterbrand to products (Figure 3.2). A multi-country, cross-category team working on the Knorr food brand used this approach to develop its global vision. The breakthrough came by getting people to ditch their current

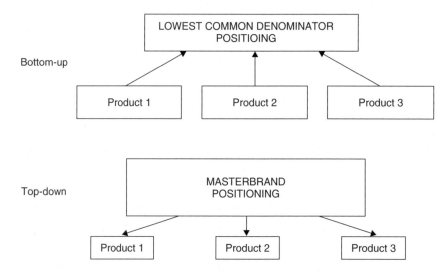

Figure 3.2: Different approaches to brand vision.

product- or market-based viewpoints and work together on a new, future-focused idea for the brand. They were encouraged to act as the board of the Knorr company rather than as local marketing barons and asked some challenging questions:

- What sort of brand did they dream of having in four or five years' time?
- What were the values they wanted to defend and fight for?
- What promise would they make if they were inventing a product range from scratch?
- What was the bigger purpose they had beyond merely selling individual products?

This process created more energy, enthusiasm and engagement than would have been achieved by starting with what was currently on the table (see Table 3.1 for more visioning process tips). A masterbrand promise about 'giving people the confidence and support to get more out of everyday food' was developed. This was brought to life with the rallying call 'more taste in your life' on the brand's website. The team then worked on the *ideal* product range to bring this idea to life. This has led to innovation such as the UK launch of Knorr Vie soups, which are enjoyably tasty but also help you get the recommended five daily portions of fruit and vegetables. In addition, other products in the Unilever portfolio that fitted the vision were rebranded as Knorr, such as the Chicken Tonight range of cook-in sauces. Finally, support was reduced or removed on older and more traditional products that did not fit as well with the vision, such as bouillon cubes and gravy mix.

Table 3.1: Vision team tips.

Overall: Experience on 50 brand visioning and positioning projects shows that many of these fail to add enough value to the business. They end up being theoretical exercises that 'go through the motions', filling in boxes but not driving a better brand mix. The following tips have been learnt from the more successful projects that *did* actually make a difference:

1. *Strong, senior leadership*: any project needs a senior person with real influence to lead it. First, they have the credibility and the experience to win over people on the team and persuade them to make compromises. Second, they have the confidence and authority to make key decisions, even when these do not please everyone.

2. *A team not a committee*: the Knorr project described earlier had a core team of only eight people, with representatives from global strategy, key markets and the two agencies. The two key criteria for the core team are business influence and added-value thinking. People who do not contribute on at least one of these levels are spectators not participants, and their input can be gathered off-line outside the key workshops.

3. *Start with the end in mind*: there should be a clear idea of how the strategy is going to drive a better brand mix. The team should know which mix development projects will be inspired and guided by the new strategy. In the case of the visioning work on Omo, one of Unilever's biggest detergent brands, the strategy project fed directly into briefs for packaging, advertising and promotion. The idea of helping children grow and develop by giving them the freedom to get dirty was quickly brought to life in communication with the tagline 'No stains, no learning'.

Positioning was covered in detail in my first book, *The Brand Gym* (1). Here, we will focus on the specific challenges and issues for a masterbrand. We will start by looking at defining your market broadly and having a point of view about the impact you want to make on this market. We will then build on this foundation with a more detailed review of masterbrand positioning, including core target, insight and brand promise. A summary of positioning tips and tricks is in Appendix 1, with definitions of tools in Appendix 2 and a detailed template in Appendix 3.

Less myopic marketing

The key first step in developing an inspiring masterbrand vision is to take a less myopic or short-sighted view of your market. Defining the market more broadly opens up your eyes to new opportunities for stretch. By not defining the market broadly enough you risk being blind to potential threats. For example, Encyclopaedia Britannica thought that it was in the book-selling business, not the learning business. The company dismissed the introduction of the Microsoft Encarta CD-ROM as it was based on a second-division encyclopaedia. Encyclopaedia Britannica persevered with its model of selling 20 superior volumes door to door at $1000 a pop. However, the consumer cared less about the depth and quality of the content and more about ease of use and a much lower price point. Encyclopaedia Britannica decided too late to extend its brand into the interactive arena. By this time its business was in almost terminal decline and Microsoft had a dominant position.

The UK board of Blockbuster is one team that discovered how redefining a market can open your mind to a much bigger, more inspiring vision for the brand.

Blockbuster: Out of the video box

For many years, Blockbuster saw itself as being in the video rental business. The sign outside the store said 'Blockbuster *Video*'. This was great when video penetration was on the up and up. However, towards the end of the 1990s the whole world of home entertainment was going through seismic change. DVD was growing rapidly as the new format for renting and buying films. Satellite, cable and broadband were multiplying the alternative channels on which people could view movies. And beyond movies, there was a literal explosion in the growth of gaming. These changes forced Blockbuster to do some hard thinking about its future.

The breakthrough idea was to redefine the competitive arena as 'the great night in' market. Video rental was clearly a key part of this. But this new definition opened the team members' minds up to other important service extensions that would have two big benefits

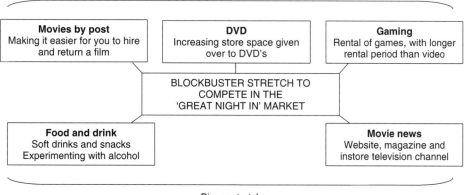

Core range extension

| **Movies by post** Making it easier for you to hire and return a film | **DVD** Increasing store space given over to DVD's | **Gaming** Rental of games, with longer rental period than video |

BLOCKBUSTER STRETCH TO COMPETE IN THE 'GREAT NIGHT IN' MARKET

| **Food and drink** Soft drinks and snacks Experimenting with alcohol | **Movie news** Website, magazine and instore television channel |

Bigger stretch

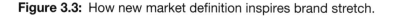

Figure 3.3: How new market definition inspires brand stretch.

(Figure 3.3). First, they would enhance the great night in experience, increasing satisfaction with Blockbuster. Second, they would generate new revenue streams.

The most basic move was to promote DVD aggressively as a core range extension, giving this format a share of store space ahead of its share of market. This had benefits in terms of superior film quality, but also store utilization owing to the thinner format. Video game rental has also been introduced to capitalize on the explosive growth of this market, now bigger than movies and music combined.

Further extensions stretched beyond the core to other aspects of a great night in. Complementary products such as soft drinks, salty snacks and ice creams are on sale at the check-out. The brand is also starting to offer services such as a movie magazine to help you choose the right film for you. On the staff side, the firm is also trying to hire people for the store who are really interested in movies and so able to give face-to-face advice that can help you have a great night in.

> ## Blockbuster summary
>
> 1. Be less myopic about your market.
> 2. Think what bigger promise you could make based on this broader definition.
> 3. Translate this promise into ideas for core range extension and bigger stretch.

Climbing the brand ladder

The Blockbuster story shows how a broader market definition can help you develop a bigger masterbrand idea to stimulate development of new extension ideas. The process of looking for a bigger, broader benefit area is sometimes called 'laddering'. This involves asking the question 'why?' several times, a bit like an inquisitive toddler. The Blockbuster team asked why renting a video was really important and found that it was an integral part of delivering a great night in. Blockbuster started to transform itself from a video rental library into a 'great night in provider'. This idea in turn helped generate new ideas for stretching, such as new movie formats and complementary usage products such as food and drink.

We will now see how market redefinition can be the foundation for a new and inspiring masterbrand vision, by looking at the relaunch of the Pampers brand.

Pampers: From bottoms to babies

After 40 years focused on nappies (diapers) and dryness protection, at the end of the 1990s the Pampers team developed a bigger, bolder vision. This new vision (see Figure 3.4 for my stab at the masterbrand positioning) has inspired and guided a transformation of the whole brand mix, including communication to parents, product offerings and direct marketing. Extensions of the core nappy range have boosted share in the UK by over 10 per cent and stretch into adjacent markets has added on new business worth over $150 million.

Drilling for nuggets

As with Blockbuster, the first challenge for the team members was opening their eyes to a broader *market definition*. They quickly concluded that diapers were in fact only one, albeit important, part of 'helping keep a baby's delicate skin protected and healthy'. The brand had the potential to do much more for parents in this area, as shown by the success that some markets had already achieved with baby wipes. With the idea of healthy, protected skin in mind, work started on drilling for new nuggets of insight.

To focus the insight work, the *core target* was tightly defined to develop a vivid and colourful picture of the Pampers user. This avoided the common mistake of having a broad masterbrand target that tries to cover the whole market and so ends up being vague, bland and uninspiring. For Pampers, the core target was a mum who was actively interested in her child's development and wanted to learn more to understand how to become a better parent. A broader *consumption target*, including dads and second-time mums, is attracted to the brand as those involved aspire to the same core values (Figure 3.5).

Extensive research with this core target was complemented by internal discussions and interviews with child experts. A series of 'insight drills' was employed to ask questions such as 'Why is healthy skin really important?' and 'What happens when products work well

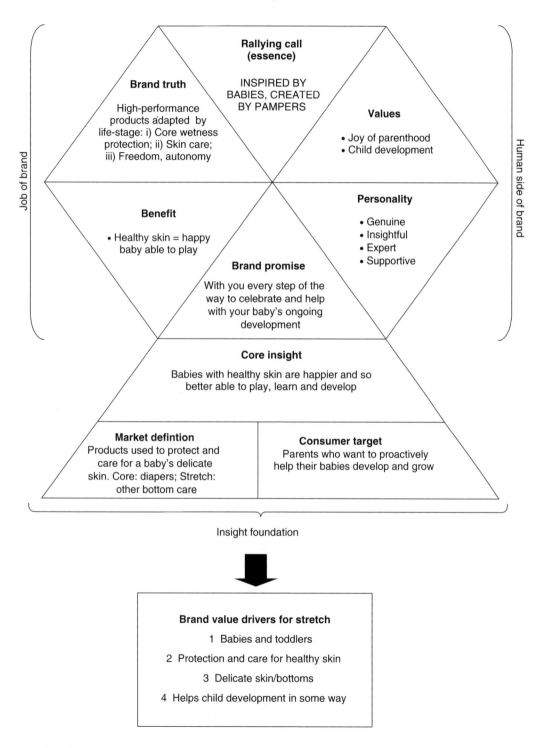

Figure 3.4: Pampers' masterbrand vision (author's own).

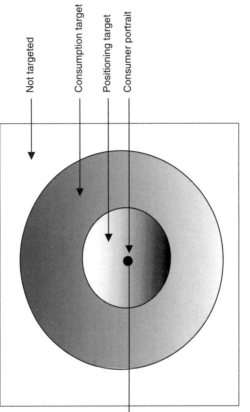

Not targeted

Consumption target

Positioning target

Consumer portrait

Attitudes to life
Guiding principles
that influence approach
to life in general
(e.g. ambitious, live
life for today, concern
for environment)

Needs
Functional and emotional
needs from the category
(e.g. refreshment, status,
indulgence)

Interest centres
What they like to spend
their time and money on
(e.g. exotic holidays,
gadgets, sport)

Sociodemographics
Centre of gravity of group
in terms of age, sex,
social class etc.

Figure 3.5: Consumer targets.

and when they fail?' This work helped uncover a new and powerful *insight*: 'healthy skin is important for a happy baby to be able to play, learn and develop'. This was fresher, more contemporary and more inspiring than the old insight ('parents feel guilty when their babies get wet, as this often leads to nappy rash'). The ultimate *brand promise*, the most persuasive reason for choosing Pampers, was 'With you every step of the way to celebrate and help you with your baby's ongoing development'.

This new positioning avoided the risk with masterbrands of developing a strategy that is fat and flabby in an attempt to cover every possible product extension. Pampers took a clear and confident stance in focusing on child development. This helped the positioning perform well against the three key criteria for evaluating such a strategy (Figure 3.6):

- *Motivating*: the promise of giving you the confidence that you are caring for your baby's development was a big idea with an emotional component. This made it motivating for consumers, but also inspiring for the brand team. However, this promise was underpinned by a clear functional *benefit* of 'healthy skin = happy baby able to play, learn and develop'. In other words, there was some sausage and not just sizzle.
- *Different*: the emphasis on child development was very different to the more light-hearted and playful positioning of key competitor Huggies. It had a further advantage of being hard to copy by less expert retailer own-label diaper brands.

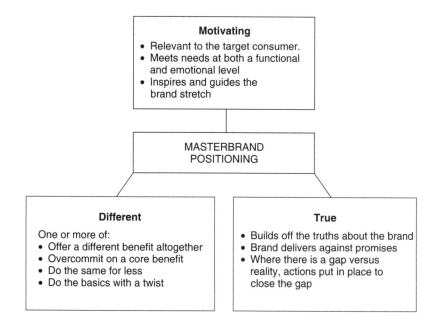

Figure 3.6: Masterbrand positioning criteria.

- *True*: the positioning was supported by some clear product *truths* via high-performance products. The basic 'Baby Dry' diaper range already provided superior dryness protection. In addition, innovative new brand extensions were key to dramatizing the new vision.

New tools for the job

Brand stretch translated the Pampers promise into new products (Figure 3.7) that did more to help parents care for their young children's delicate skin. The bigger and bolder vision

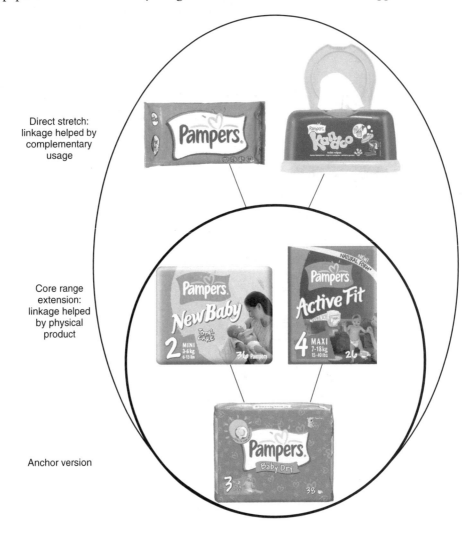

Direct stretch:
linkage helped by
complementary
usage

Core range
extension:
linkage helped
by physical
product

Anchor version

Figure 3.7: Pampers' stretch sticking to idea of caring and protecting delicate skin.

inspired and guided both extension on the core business and stretch into new areas that would have been less likely with the old, dryness-focused positioning:

- *Core nappy business*: this is where work started. A new range of premium-priced diapers was designed to meet the needs of babies at different stages of development. For example, 'New Baby' was specially developed for (ugh) runny poo that comes from a liquid diet. 'Active Fit' has extra stretchy sides to provide a perfect fit when the baby is older and on the move (a baby can crawl up to a quarter of a mile in 20 minutes; no wonder parents are worn out all the time). These new extensions clearly dramatized the brand's understanding of baby development *and* the use of this in developing products. In the 18 months following the 2001 relaunch, market share grew strongly from 47 to 55 per cent, driven by the premium-priced new extensions.
- *Stretch into toddler care*: this was achieved with the launch of Kandoo, a moist and flushable toilet wipe in an impactful and easy-to-use dispenser. Again, this is a great manifestation of the brand's baby development promise, by helping young children gain independence in their attempts to use the 'big toilet'. The advertising showed how a young boy became 'King of the throne' thanks to Pampers Kandoo. The product is supported by the brand's product benefit of cleaning and caring for skin. This extension has exceeded all sales targets and is now four times bigger than the nearest competitor, Johnson & Johnson Extra Clean. Along with the existing baby wipes extensions, this new business has provided over $150 million of incremental business.

From expert mother to mum's friend

The second big part of bringing the vision to life was to define and communicate the human side of the brand: its values and personality. For many years brand communication showcased 'expert mothers' such as creche supervisors and paediatricians authoritatively telling mum that Pampers knew best. New *values* defined the guiding principles and beliefs that would produce a more collaborative relationship between Pampers and the parent:

- *Celebrating the joy* of the mother and baby relationship, rather than hammering home the risks and worries.
- *Child development*: Pampers would invest in really understanding how children develop at each stage of their life and sharing this knowledge with you.

Pampers' *personality* also evolved in an attempt to create a closer bond with the consumer. Pampers would also gain insights into the world through the eyes of the baby and use this knowledge to show a more genuine and positive portrayal of babies. This is in contrast with competitor Huggies, whose communication shows babies dressed up like grown-ups in an attempt to create humorous advertising. This idea is reflected in the shorthand summary of the brand's positioning, a *rallying call* of 'Inspired by babies. Created by Pampers.' This is used as a communication endline, but it is also a great call to action for the Pampers team. (Don't worry about using an ad slogan as your rallying call/essence if it captures the brand idea in two or three words, even if this is against the textbook rules. The key is to find not clever words that sum up why you succeeded in the past, but a phrase that inspires and guides the team into the future.)

The new personality of the Pampers brand is reflected in a new brand logo and identity that are bright, optimistic and contemporary. This is a big change from the old identity, which featured a more traditional and almost doll-like baby image (Figure 3.8). It would have been much harder to launch exciting new extensions such as Kandoo with the old face of Pampers.

Brand dialogue

Direct marketing has also been redesigned to promote the new vision and range. Mailings to 95 per cent of UK mums are timed to coincide with key stages in the baby's

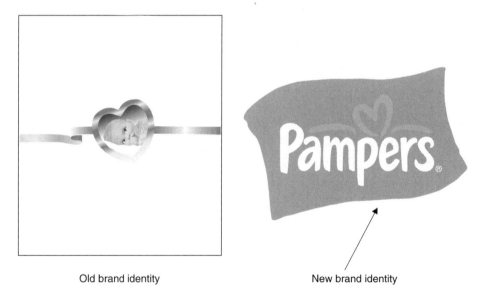

Old brand identity   New brand identity

Figure 3.8: Newer, fresher and more modern brand identity.

Source: Product images reproduced by permission of Procter & Gamble.

development. They include useful booklets written by child experts and coupons for the most appropriate product in the range. The Pampers.com website was relaunched to be less of a product catalogue and more a source of helpful advice around the clock. Over 400,000 people now visit the site every month. An opt-in email system allows the brand to have further communication with parents at key stages of baby development, again using a combination of helpful advice and promotion of targeted products.

Remember what made you famous

Pampers has succeeded in using direct stretch to go from being a product brand focused on dryness to become a child development specialist focused on baby care. Interestingly, this means that the brand has stopped short of creating a healthy skin umbrella platform to enter more distant markets, such as baby shampoo and bath products. The technology for these extensions exists in P&G, but the team currently believes that this could be a brand ego trip. Pampers' expertise is still linked to delicate skin (i.e. bottoms). In addition, there is a strong competitor in Johnson & Johnson, for whom bath products are a core business. Taking on J&J would not be impossible, but for now P&G believes that the investment needed will deliver a better return on the core business and more direct stretching.

Defining a series of *brand value drivers* can help guide the type of stretch on which your brand could focus. One way to generate these drivers is to ask yourself 'What made us famous in the first place?' and 'What is really driving value for our consumers?' For Pampers this could lead to the following:

- Babies and toddlers.
- Protection and care for healthy skin.
- Delicate skin/bottoms.
- Help child development in at least a small way.

This question of how far a brand can *profitably* stretch is a key one for every masterbrand to ask. Too much stretch too soon can be expensive and unrewarding, a lesson learnt the hard way by Axe body spray for men (called Lynx in the UK).

Pampers summary

1. A tight core target and deep insight lead to a more powerful positioning.
2. Try to build off a clear product truth when stretching.
3. Ask what made you famous and use the answer to guide extension efforts.

Axe: Ladders and snakes

At the end of the 1990s, Axe undertook a highly ambitious and at the time widely acclaimed programme of brand stretch. The brand had already used direct stretch from its core body spray into shower gel, with the brand linkage of fragrance. Additional indirect extension followed over a frenetic 12-month period. Shampoo and hair-styling products were introduced and Axe even went head to head with the mighty Gillette in its core market, through a joint venture with one of Japan's leading shaver manufacturers. Axe also spotted a gap in the hairdressing market: if a young boy wanted a haircut he had to choose between the old-fashioned local barber or a unisex salon. Axe barbershops would offer a lad's paradise, with video games, men's magazines and sexy girls to cut your hair. Two branches were opened, one on Oxford Street in London and the other in Kingston, Surrey. A couple of years on and many millions of dollars later, little is left to show for all this activity. All but one of the extensions has been withdrawn and the barber shops have become burger bars. What went wrong?

Up the ladder...

This stretching was based on a market definition that was dramatically expanded from 'body spray' to 'male grooming'. This led to a new masterbrand idea of 'Grooms men to seduce'. The linkage between the different product platforms and the core, the brand glue if you like, was the brand's distinctive and highly motivating emotional values and personality. Unlike competitors such as Gillette, Axe did not take itself seriously. The stars of Axe adverts were anti-heroes: they made fun of themselves and looked anything but cool. However, it was this irreverent, streetwise and entertaining approach that made the brand so appealing.

... and down a snake

With the benefit of hindsight, male grooming was too wide a market definition and the promise of 'grooms men to seduce' was a few too many rungs up the ladder; as in the board game, the brand hit a snake and slid down. It entered markets where it lacked the functional competence to win (Figure 3.9), leaving it with only emotional values to lean on. And as we saw earlier with Virgin, all sizzle and no sausage is rarely enough to win. Even one of the brand's best-performing adverts of all time could not save the shaving extension. It lacked the technical credibility to compete effectively with Gillette, who spent hundreds of millions of dollars on R&D and marketing support. The hair care market is also highly competitive and Axe lacked the cleaning and caring credentials to get men to ditch their Head & Shoulders

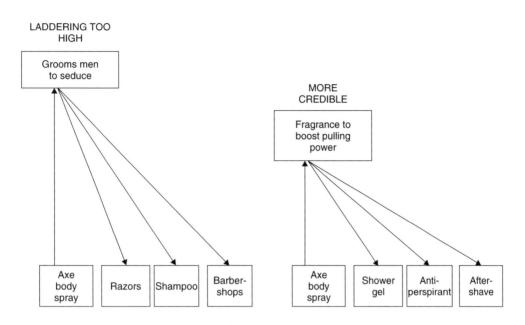

Figure 3.9: Ladders and snakes for Axe.

or Pantene. The failure of the barbershops showed that execution is the key to retail success, with a good concept merely the visible tip of the iceberg.

A more realistic idea is 'fragrances to boost your pulling power'. With this idea the brand has been able to use direct stretch beyond body sprays into shower gel, which has been successful in some markets. Here, the brand's fragrance credentials are a real added-value brand linkage. The brand's personality has inspired certain variants that emphasize the emotional lift that Axe gives you. The Re-load version provides extra energy for a night out,

> **Axe summary**
>
> 1. Too wide a market definition leads to an ego trip.
> 2. A great personality won't save a poor product.
> 3. Building new competences is hard, especially going from products to services or vice versa.

while the Sunrise version helps you get over a hangover the morning after! This broader promise can also support anti-persperant deodorant and aftershave.

However, the team has been smart enough to recognize the hard truth that the biggest source of profitable growth is the core body spray business. Even better brand communication, improved fragrances, upgraded packaging and broader distribution are now top of the agenda. These projects might be less sexy than entering totally new markets such as shaving, but they are likely to deliver a much better return on investment.

Elastic brands

Research by the brandgym suggests that despite the risks, many marketing teams have ambitions to stretch far from the core. Core range extension is expected to account for only 46 per cent of extensions in the next three years, down from 63 per cent in the past three years (Figure 3.10). Instead, more use of direct and indirect stretch is planned. However, many of these brands may actually lack the suppleness to stretch this far, at least in a way that delivers a decent return on investment.

Before you decide to work on bigger stretch into adjacent or distant markets, you may want to use the following 'brand typologies' (Table 3.2) to help you assess how elastic your brand is. All of these assume that the brand and core product have been strengthened, as discussed in the last chapter.

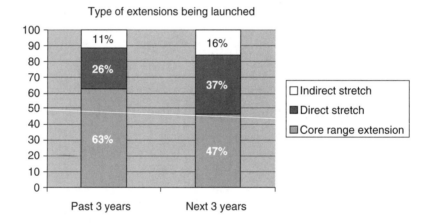

Figure 3.10: Increasing use of bigger stretch.

Table 3.2: Suppleness check.

	Coca-Cola	Head & Shoulders	Pampers	Axe	Dove	Virgin	Gucci	Cosmo	YOUR BRAND?
1 Open versus closed name	***	*	***	***	***	***	***	***	
2 Attribute flexibility	0	0	**	**	**	***	***	**	
3 Benefit flexibility	*	0	**	**	***	***	***	***	
4 Badge values	*	0	0	*	0	0	***	**	
TYPOLOGY	Product brand		Specialist brand		Umbrella brand		Lifestyle brand		?

The product brand: Focus on core range extension

This brand has the lowest level of suppleness and should stick to core range extension or even no extension at all. At the most basic level, it may have a *'closed' rather than 'open' name* that makes it harder to stretch. For example, Shredded Wheat will struggle to sell something that is not shredded and made from wheat. British Gas is slowly making inroads into the UK electricity market, but a good deal of money and time have been needed merely to get over the first hurdle. In contrast, a made-up name with no inherent meaning like Yahoo!, Virgin or Egg leaves more flexibility for brand extension.

A more fundamental issue concerns *attribute flexibility*. Suppleness is limited by strong associations with particular attributes, such as colour, taste or shape (2). This is especially true for brands that define a particular product category, in the way that Pepsi and Coke are the definitive colas. This makes it hard to do even core range extensions that break the brand's codes without confusing consumers and so running the risk of low trial. For example, 7-Up failed when it tried to break out of the lime and lemon category, of which it was the definitive brand. The failure of 7-Up Gold was explained by one executive as follows:

> The product was misunderstood by the consumer. People had a clear view of what 7Up products should be – clear and crisp, clean and no caffeine. 7-Up Gold is darker and it does have caffeine and so doesn't fit the 7-Up image (3).

Breaking out of a perception straitjacket is of course made harder by remaining a mono-product offer for years, decades or even centuries, in the case of Coca-Cola. As with people, lack of stretching causes a brand's muscles to atrophy and lose suppleness. In contrast, the more a brand stretches, the easier it becomes to stretch further.

The specialist brand: Focus on direct stretch

Unlike the product brand, the specialist is not held back by strong associations with specific attributes such as format and colour. However, the specialist brand's strength is famous for its expertise and focus and so when stretching it stays close to the core. It can achieve direct stretch into adjacent categories that are close to the core in terms of consumer perception. For example, Colgate has stretched from toothpaste to offer a range of complementary products that deliver oral care benefits, including toothbrushes, oral care chewing gum and mouthwash (Figure 3.11).

In some cases brands learn the hard way that they are specialist brands that are better off sticking to a more tightly defined, functional promise. Domestos has refocused on being a specialist in germ kill for toilets, building on its heritage as a bleach that 'Kills 99% of all known germs – dead'. This follows limited success at creating an umbrella concept around

Figure 3.11: Complementing the core.

Reproduced by permission of Colgate Palmolive.

'home hygiene', with extensions going outside the toilet and into products such as cleaning wipes for household surfaces. The team has decided that what really works on Domestos is being a simple, straightforward and highly effective problem solver. More success has been achieved with direct stretch into toilet gels that deliver germ kill plus limescale removal and cleaning (Figure 3.12). In 2003 the brand also relaunched its core bleach range with a thicker, more effective product.

The umbrella brand: Focus on indirect stretch

This brand is much more supple because it has a promise with potential to serve as an umbrella concept for more distant markets that don't have direct link to the core. The UK supermarket Tesco's idea of 'Every little helps' has stretched beyond the core area of food to include other products and services that offer high quality, accessible prices and convenience. A Tesco shopper can buy videos, clothes, petrol and even financial services.

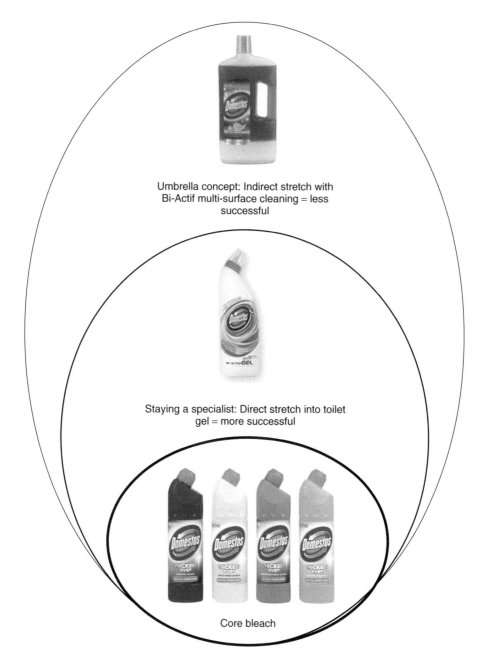

Umbrella concept: Indirect stretch with
Bi-Actif multi-surface cleaning = less
successful

Staying a specialist: Direct stretch into toilet
gel = more successful

Core bleach

Figure 3.12: Domestos extensions.

Product images reproduced by permission of Lever Fabergé.

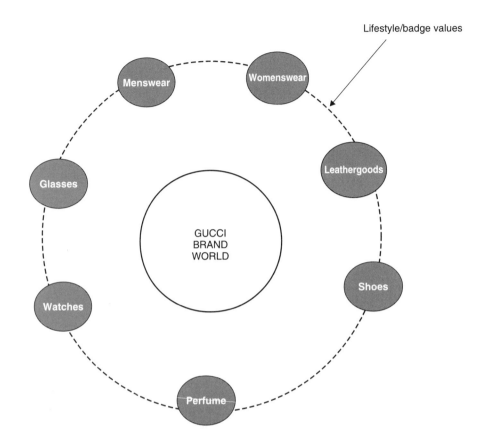

Figure 3.13: 360° stretch of a lifestyle brand.

The first supermarket extension into banking in the mid-1990s was seen by many as a no-hoper, as one branding expert from the Henley Centre commented: 'Sainsbury is trying to make a big jump in one go. I would worry it was a step too far' (4). This extension now has 1.4 million customers and in 2002 operating profit was £22 million, up 66 per cent year on year (5). In contrast, it would be much harder for Barclay's bank to start selling groceries in its branches, as it is much more of a specialist brand.

The lifestyle brand: 360° stretch

If you are one of the rare brands that has 'badge values', you are the most supple of all. These aspirational and emotional values provide the glue to tie together a disperse range of products. People are effectively paying to be part of the Gucci 'club', whether they are buying a t-shirt, handbag or motorbike helmet (Figure 3.13). Brands with these values are more likely to be found in luxury goods or fashion than pasta sauce or potato chips.

 **Key takeouts**

1. Having a clear and challenging vision for the masterbrand helps stimulate the creation of big, bold ideas for brand stretch.
2. A broader market definition is the foundation of such a vision.
3. Care needs to be taken when laddering up to a bigger idea, to ensure that this is credible and not a brand ego trip.

Checklist 3: Vision

	Yes	No
• Are you working top down on the masterbrand vision, not bottom up?	☐	☐
• Have you defined your market in broad, benefit terms, not narrow manufacturer ones?	☐	☐
• Have you brought to life a rich, vivid picture of your *core* positioning target?	☐	☐
• Are you clear about what made your brand famous in the first place?	☐	☐
• When laddering up to a bigger brand promise, have you avoided brand ego tripping by being credible and motivating?	☐	☐
• Is the positioning sharp and focused, not fat and flabby?	☐	☐
• Have you done a reality check on the suppleness of your brand to guide your extension efforts?	☐	☐

Handover

We have now seen how a clear and ambitious vision for the brand can serve as a stimulus for stretch. We have also looked at the need to be realistic about the suppleness of your brand and the most appropriate form of stretch on which to focus. With this in mind, we will now move on to see how specific insights into people, brands and markets can be used as the catalyst for generating brand stretch ideas.

Step Three: Ideas

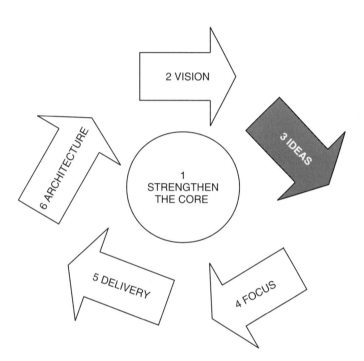

 ## Headlines

With a clear and inspiring vision in place, the next step is to use this for generating extension ideas. This should start with a search for opportunities to extend the core range, using a number of different insight springboards. Importantly, consumers are only one source of ideas. Many successful extensions come from borrowing ideas from competitors and companies in other categories, or looking within the company itself. Whatever the source of insight, be ready to work not in the neat and tidy fairytale world of innovation, but in the real one. Here, 'innokill' will be a key barrier to jump over or bash your way through on the way to launching a new extension.

Start close to home

Extending the core range might be less sexy than a bigger stretch into new markets. However, it strengthens the foundations on which the brand is built and can also be a good source of growth.

Before you extend

Importantly, extension is merely one way of growing the core business and should only be done after other avenues have been fully optimized, such as:

- Core product/pack or service.
- Distribution.
- Pricing.
- Communication.
- Sizing and size by channel.
- Promotion.

Kellogg's Cornflakes is an example of a brand that seems to have recognized the importance of nurturing the core product. After having spent several years focused on extensions, in 2003 the brand put a big push behind upgrading the core pack, foil wrapping the cereal for better freshness.

Core range extension

If the core product mix has been optimized, attention can turn to core range extension. This can involve new versions that introduce a new *flavour* or *functional benefit*. For example, the Sida haircare brand in Brazil launched a hydrating shampoo especially for 'mulatto' or mixed race hair. This was a key part of the brand's repositioning as one that really understood Brazilian women, which trebled sales between 1997 and 1999.

The other main type of core range extension is format change. This can be through *modifying the product format* to better meet the needs of consumers. For example, over 50 million bars of Kit Kat Chunky were despatched within the first few weeks of its launch. Within six months more than 20 per cent of the UK population had tried the product and the repeat rates were high (1). This extension helped address declining usage among 12–20-year-olds, who liked the wafer texture of the original four-finger Kit Kat but wanted a more substantial and satisfying eat.

Format change can also be through *new pack formats*, which can be highly effective when they address real needs. 'Thinking big' led Coke to develop 1.5l PET bottles that boosted in-home consumption. 'Thinking small' inspired Pringles to launch mini cans that opened up a whole new eating moment for individuals on the move and boosted the price per unit.

Market mapping

Analysing brand performance against six dimensions that drive consumer choice can help identify core range extension opportunities: people, periods, places, purpose, price and product. The performance of the brand is reviewed against each of these '6 P's' to highlight areas of 'underlap' where the brand is underperforming. Extension is one way of filling these gaps (Figure 4.1). The six dimensions are of course all interrelated, but looking at each of them in turn usually does throw up different ideas.

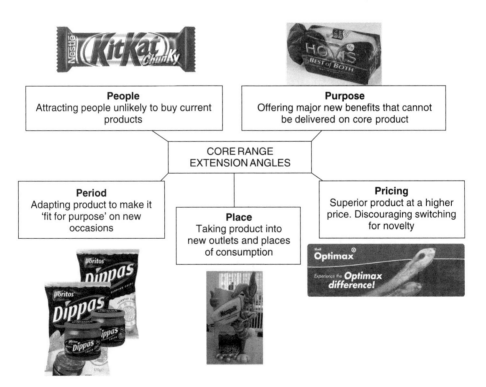

Figure 4.1: Core range extension angles.

People: New users

Levi's Engineered Jeans (LEJ) played a key role in the brand's successful drive to win back younger people. This key target group had deserted the brand during the 1990s, leading to a decline in share from 30 to 14 per cent. Product range was a key weakness, as the marketing director for northern Europe described:

> The traditional 501s were still a huge seller, but we rode too long on that glory. We suddenly started to lose customers, particularly the 15–19-year-olds who had switched to cargo and combat pants. Levi's weren't cool or sexy any more (2).

Some observers went as far as proclaiming that 'denim was dead'. However, with LEJ Levi's was able to reinvent its core product for a whole new generation. The product had a twisted seam that made jeans more comfortable to wear but also made them look new and different. Share of 11–24-year-olds grew by 9 per cent during the first year of launch and LEJ became 11–12 per cent of the brand's business.

Rejuvenating the user base is not just important for fashion brands. Polaroid was a brand in risk of losing relevance to younger people, who no longer found the idea of instant photos that exciting. The new I-Zone camera has helped recruit these younger users into the brand. The colourful product design and more portable format fit their needs (Figure 4.2). The smaller-format photos are ideal for sticking on locker doors and on exercise pads and books. Distribution in new channels such as supermarkets and toy shops helped launch the extension.

Purpose: New benefits

Another extension angle is to deliver a new benefit, as Hovis did in the UK with its core range extension 'Best of Both'. This met the need of mums to 'smuggle in' the goodness of

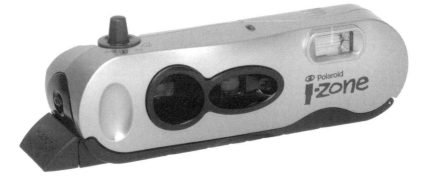

Figure 4.2: Polaroid I-Zone.

Reproduced by permission of Polaroid Corp.

wholemeal bread, for which Hovis was famous, in a white bread that was more acceptable to children. This new product was a key part of the brand's 30 per cent growth between 1999 and 2001. It also helped Hovis gain a stronger position in the key white bread segment, where it had previously been a minor player.

Periods: New occasions

Looking at brand usage by occasion can highlight extension opportunities, especially when product choice is strongly influenced by the moment of consumption, as in food. The UK team working on Doritos corn chips found that the company was underrepresented in the key evening moment, typically when a group of family or friends are munching in front of the television. The Doritos Dippas extension, a range of oversized corn chips and accompanying dips, was positioned to boost usage in the evening. Advertising with the inspired tagline of 'Friendchips' reinforced the idea of relaxed social sharing with friends. Sales rose by 76 per cent versus the previous year, with total sales of the Doritos brand rising by 13 per cent. The successful strategy was rolled out to other markets, including Belgium, the Netherlands and Spain (3).

Places: New channels

Extension can also involve taking the brand into new channels and so increasing the number of usage opportunities. The children's drink brand Nesquik started out as a powder to be mixed with milk. It has stretched to offer a ready-to-drink version through installing 1000 'bunny' machines in the UK out-of-home market. This added an incremental $7.5 million of sales in the first year of launch (4).

Price: Premiumization

A premium offer can be a good way of generating incremental profit *if* the price is justified by real consumer benefits, as in the case of Shell Optimax. Fierce price competition from UK supermarkets and reduced support from the major brand owners had led to consumers seeing petrol as a commodity. However, Shell identified a segment of 'real driver' consumers who were genuinely interested in boosting car performance and ready to pay more for this. Shell Optimax offered better acceleration and engine care at a 5 per cent premium versus standard unleaded petrol. This may not sound much, but it makes a big difference when margins are cut to the bone. The extension was rolled out to all 1100 Shell service stations and backed with an $8 million marketing campaign encouraging drivers to switch to Shell Optimax. The launch succeeded in boosting margins and attracting new users and the investment paid back in just eight months versus a target of 15 months (5).

After working on core range extensions, idea generation can look for possible opportunities to stretch beyond the core.

Moving out

There are several different ways into the development of ideas for stretching beyond the core. These include insight into consumer-led, market-led and innovation-led opportunities. As with core range extension idea generation, these three areas all overlap, but considering each in turn may throw up different thoughts.

Consumer-led

Thinking about the broader needs of your consumer beyond the core product or service can stimulate ideas for stretching:

- *Total, end-to-end customer experience*: Blockbuster developed ideas to complement the core movie offering, such as food, drinks and a movie magazine.
- *Consumer life stages*: Pampers considered how children developed at each life stage, leading to the launch of Kandoo toddler toilet wipes.
- *Consumer lifestyle*: Apple really understands how personal computers have become the 'hub' for a range of activities such as digital music and digital photography. This led to the development of new iPhoto and iMovies software and the creation of the iPod music player.

Market-led

Another idea-generation technique is to review adjacent markets close to the one served by the core product. Consumers can help in identifying market opportunities, suggesting products that feel like close family members (i.e. adjacent markets) and others that are more distant cousins. The team can then consider different ways of delivering the brand benefit in these new markets (Figure 4.3).

Product truth

The most obvious linkage from core to new markets is where a brand has a transportable core product truth. Pantene has extended from shampoo into hair-styling products that also make the hair 'so healthy it shines', thanks to the brand's Provitamin ingredient. We saw earlier in the book how Dove has also gone down this route by using its 1/4 moisturizing cream truth as a linkage when stretching into new markets.

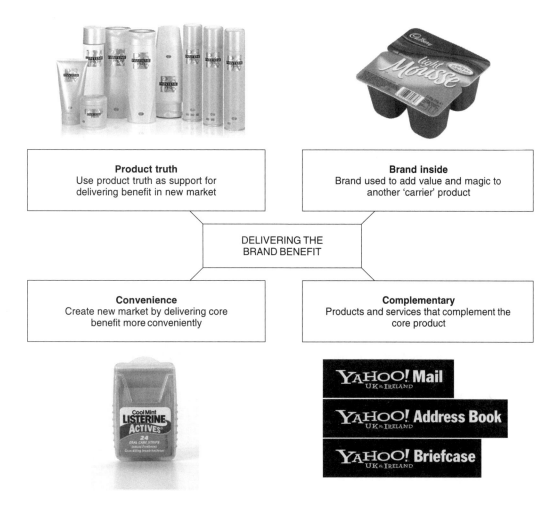

Figure 4.3: Angles to stretch beyond the core.

Pantene packshot reproduced by permission of Procter & Gamble; Cadbury's mousse packshot reproduced by permission of Cadbury Ltd; Listerine packshot reproduced by permission of Pfizer Consumer Healthcare; Yahoo! logos reproduced by permission of Yahoo Inc.

In service branding the Virgin story showed how the promise of being an irreverent fighter for value was used to stretch into distant markets such as financial services. Here, the brand truth is not an ingredient, but rather the Virgin culture and people, led from the top by Richard Branson.

Brand inside

One way of delivering the brand's benefit in new markets is to use the whole brand, not merely the product truth, as an added-value ingredient. This is a common strategy in food and drinks, where brands can provide a well-recognized and appreciated taste. Cadbury's has stretched from chocolate bars into cream desserts and ice cream. Importantly, the strong image of Cadbury's core Dairy Milk chocolate bar means that the taste perception of the extensions is better than if any old chocolate had been used. Other examples of this route are Mars drinks, Smirnoff Ice and Smarties desserts.

Complementary usage

Another way of looking for stretch opportunities is to consider products and services that complement the core offer. For example, Yahoo! encourages its email subscribers also to use linked services such as an address book and online briefcase to deepen the brand–consumer relationship. Service brands like Yahoo! have the huge benefit of large and regular consumer traffic that can be easily and cheaply exposed to new extension ideas. In the product arena, Gillette shave gel and Colgate toothbrushes are examples of this route.

Lifestyle and badge values

For this elite group of brands the stretch boundaries are much bigger and idea generation is much more flexible. The list of markets into which the brand could stretch is almost limitless. The key challenge here is to ensure that the right level of quality is maintained in order to retain brand integrity. The Gucci brand was almost killed in the 1980s when it was slapped onto 22 000 different products, many low priced and low quality. The arrival of Tom Ford as creative director changed all this. He took direct responsibility for approving every Gucci extension, from handbags to perfume, and also dramatically cut back the number of items on sale.

Innovation-led

Stretch does not *have* to involve entering an existing market. It can also be used to create a new market, by delivering an existing benefit in a more convenient form. Listerine 'Pocket Paks' ('Actives' in the UK) have created a whole new business worth over $100 million in the USA (6). The micro-thin, postage stamp-sized films deliver the germ kill action of Listerine mouthwash in a portable and discreet format that melts on the tongue. Another example of new category creation is the launch of disposable household cleaning wipes from brands like Cif. These are quick and easy to use and avoid the need to have smelly, dirty cloths hanging around your house.

The extension angles we have looked at so far provide a good consumer- and market-led framework for identifying extension opportunities. However, in reality perhaps only half or less of successful innovations originate in this way. Often, extension ideas come by using 'innovation shortcuts' that save time and money (Figure 4.4).

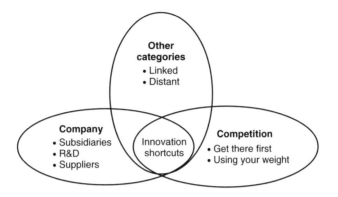

Figure 4.4: Innovation shortcuts.

Innovation shortcuts

Other categories

Copying the codes from other, more aspirational categories can be a great source of ideas. Solero borrowed codes from carbonated soft drinks to develop its new extensions (Figure 4.5): Shots (small balls of ice) and Smoover (a pouch of flavoured crushed ice). These extensions have created incremental volume by taking sales not from other ice lollies in the chiller cabinet, but from carbonated soft drinks. They have also allowed the brand to attract younger users. These extensions were inspired by a programme of 'undercover' research to

Figure 4.5: Copying codes from other categories.

Reproduced by permission of Unilever plc.

observe young people consuming soft drinks. This study highlighted several weaknesses that the extensions needed to address:

- *Put-downability*: a bottle of soft drink can be put down on the floor or a nearby surface while you chat with friends. An ice lolly has to be eaten in one go.
- *Swigging not sucking*: the swigging motion of a soft drink mimics grown-up drinking codes. In contrast, ice lollies are sucked, a regressive gesture that reminds you of childhood.
- *Clean is cool*: soft drinks are clean whereas ice lollies are messy, another unwanted reminder of being a baby.

These issues were addressed by innovative new packaging and product textures delivering new and exciting in-mouth experiences. For Shots, a cone-shaped pack with a flat bottom and resealable top meant that the product could be put down like a can or bottle. The product was swigged not sucked, just like a soft drink. For Smoover, the pack mimicked the pouch codes of sports drinks.

Your own company

Technical treasure hunt

In many companies the ivory tower syndrome means that marketing teams fail to access the talent and ideas in other departments. However, asking the guys in research and development to show you their pet projects can pay off substantially. On the Solero Shots project we saw earlier, a critical turning point was when the Spanish R&D head turned up as a surprise guest to a brainstorming session. He brought a bag of unusual-looking mini ice balls, the size of small ball bearings. A handful of these could be thrown into the mouth at once, creating a mouth feel a little like the bubbles of a soft drink. They became the product that was launched. Importantly, this product idea was not created as a formal part of the stretch project based on a brief. It had been developed by experimenting with dropping ice into liquid nitrogen, just for the hell of it.

Import ideas

Looking at what teams from your company in other markets are doing is another simple but often overlooked source of ideas. Many of the most creative new product ideas come from individual markets experimenting locally, rather than from huge, multi-country innovation projects. One of McDonald's most successful new extensions, Deluxe Potatoes, was initially developed and launched by the team in the Netherlands. The product was a big hit and was presented at a regular idea-exchange meeting of European marketing directors, where it was picked up and exported to other markets. The other major extension successes for McDonald's, such as the Hot Apple Pie and Filet o' Fish, have also come from local markets rather than head office; the latter has been the birthplace of flops such as the McLean burger and McPizza (7).

Suppliers

Suppliers can be a great source of ideas for brand extension. The CEO of Procter & Gamble, Alan Lafley, has gone as far as saying: 'I'd love to see a third to a half of "discovery" come from outside. I really want the doors open' (8). One example of where this approach has paid off is the launch of the Crest SpinBrush (Figure 4.6). This battery-powered toothbrush that retails at under $10 was originally manufactured by a small business in Cleveland, Ohio, called Dr. Johns. It had a great product, but a lack of marketing muscle to put behind it. P&G bought the business and was able to use the power of the Crest name to help provide brand credibility. This has created a whole new business worth $200 million in the USA alone.

The competition

Get there first

There can of course be a big advantage in being first to market with a new product or service, especially when two established brands are trying to extend. If you execute with excellence you have a good chance of getting a leading share of the new sector. Speed of international roll-out is increasingly important, with the challenge to be first to market in as many markets as possible. Wrigley's watched with interest the success that Listerine had in the USA with the Pocket Pak breath-freshening strips described earlier in this Workout. It created a similar products called Thin Ice and has been the first to launch this in the UK as an extension to its Extra brand of chewing gum.

Figure 4.6: Crest SpinBrush.

Reproduced by permission of Procter & Gamble.

Use your weight

Being first is not always essential for success, nevertheless. Sergio Zyman, Coke's former chief marketing officer, calls strong brands entering late to a new market 'insurgent incumbents'. They can let new brands create a functional understanding of the new category and then follow up with similar or better products plus the weight of an established brand name and image. Better and bigger distribution, pricing and marketing support are additional sources of advantage.

For example, Kettle Chips created and built up over many years an up-market, premium-priced potato chip segment. The brand offered gourmet flavours and a thicker, crunchier, 'home-made'-style texture. The leading potato chip brand in the UK, Frito-Lay's Walkers, finally launched a range to compete with Kettle Chips in 2001. Walkers' Sensations had packaging featuring high-quality black-and-white photography (Figure 4.7) and were

Figure 4.7: Insurgent incumbent.

Reproduced by permission of Walkers Snacks.

positioned as 'Posh chips from Walkers'. The recipes were more exotic than run-of-the-mill crisps. Instead of cheese and onion or ready salted, the offer included a Sea Salt and Cracked Black Pepper flavour as well as Thai Sweet Chilli. Slightly higher pricing and smaller pack sizes meant that they were sold at about a 10 per cent price premium per gram versus the core Walkers range. Frito-Lay's distribution and point-of-sale presence have been powerful weapons against the much smaller Kettle Chips. The brand extension achieved its annual sales target in only three months and television advertising was temporarily stopped after a week to control demand. Walkers Sensations have over twice the sales of Kettle Chips, at $90 million, of which 79 per cent has been incremental (9).

The fairytale world of innovation

Getting good ideas is one thing. Getting them to market is often a much bigger challenge. Most models of innovation are based on a fairytale world of innovation that sees a neat, linear process starting with consumer needs, moving smoothly into concept testing and then product development. In reality the process is more messy and iterative (Figure 4.8). Several cycles of idea generation and bags of persistence are needed, as shown by the story of Starbucks' Frappuccino.

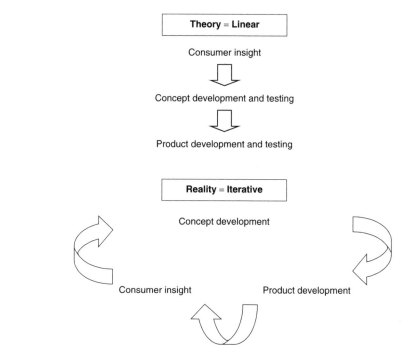

Figure 4.8: Theory and reality of brand extension innovation.

Starbucks' Frappuccino: Real world innovation

The Frappuccino extension has been a huge hit for Starbucks (Figure 4.9). It is now a $52 million business in its own right, about 7 per cent of total annual revenue (10). There are a number of real-world innovation tips that can be learnt from this successful extension.

Back your instincts

The first tip is the importance of trusting your intuition and gut. The idea for Frappuccino began in 1993 not with consumer research, but with a district manager in California who thought that an ice-based coffee drink could be a winner. She was inspired by a competitive coffee bar that was selling this sort of product. She believed sufficiently in the idea to put in place the next innovation tip and bring the idea to life.

Figure 4.9: Starbucks' Frappuccino® ice blended beverage – real-world innovation.

Reproduced by permission of Starbucks Corporation.

Bring your ideas to life

Rather than doing a PowerPoint presentation about the extension idea, the Starbucks manager experimented with a homemade blending unit. This was a great way of exploring the idea with consumers and getting initial feedback. It also helped bring the idea to life for people in the company. With the initial results, she got the support of the food and beverage team to develop a full prototype. Early in 1994 the product was sampled by the then CEO, Howard Schultz. At this point the team found out how important it was to have in place the next tool: a good crash helmet.

Get a better crash helmet

This was the advice of a general manager at P&G when I complained about 'banging my head against a brick wall' in trying to get approval for a brand extension idea. His point was that stamina, self-belief and determination were just as important as creativity and strategic thinking in getting an extension to market. The Frappuccino team had to fight hard to persuade Schultz to stick with the idea, as he hated the first product he tasted; he wanted to chuck it and the whole project down the drain. However, he was impressed enough by the commitment of the team to start on the next tip.

Think big, start small

Starbucks has the advantage of being able to experiment easily with an extension by trying it out on a small scale, as it did with Frappucccino at the end of 1994 in 12 Southern Californian stores. Direct consumer feedback from this real in-use experience helped improve the product and give enough confidence for a full, national roll-out in April of the following year.

Consumer goods companies don't have the luxury of having their own stores for testing extensions, but they can use regional tests to minimize the downside. This takes up valuable time and does give competition the chance to see what you are doing, but at least the learning is based on in-market conditions close to real life. In the past these tests have been in parts of the UK, as was the case with big hits such as Bacardi Breezer. In today's more international era the region in question might be a country.

Starbucks summary

1. Be ready to go round the innovation loop several times.
2. Think big, but start small.
3. Not everyone will share your enthusiasm: sell your idea.
4. Experimentation is the best form of research.

Innokill survival kit

Many people must dream of working in a place like Starbucks, where extensions such as Frappuccino are launched quickly and with minimal testing. However, in most big companies the early life of a brand extension is much more risky. Radical new ideas run the risk of 'innokill': being stamped to death by the results of premature and quantitatively based research. Several tricks can be used to help you maximize your chances of avoiding this fate.

Avoid premature screening

Work up your extension idea and explore it with colleagues, friends and consumers before you let the quantitative testers try and 'screen' it. Also, don't rely on a primitive line drawing, or even a written concept with no visual at all. This risks consumers not fully understanding the idea, resulting in a low 'top box' score, the percentage of people saying that they would *definitely* buy the product. Investing in a good visual and ideally a 3D prototype will pay off with better results and a bigger chance of survival. After all, imagine having researched ABS brakes as 'brakes that go on and off' or Post-it notes as 'rectangular bits of yellow paper you can stick and restick'!

The drunk and the lamppost

Avoid using research like the drunk uses a lamppost: for support not illumination. In the same way as judges on shows like *Pop Idol* have a 'nose' for a hit, brand teams need to develop their own intuition and judgement. Before doing quantitative concept research, you should have a clear point of view about the expected outcome. This is a working hypothesis that can evolve when the results come out, but these should tell you 'how high is high', not whether the idea is good or bad.

Sometimes you have to be confident enough about your own belief despite negative test results, especially when working on radical new ideas. This was the case with the successful launch of Flower by Kenzo, which helped boost the brand's sales by 75 per cent in the first six months of 2001. The chairman of parent company LVMH, Bernard Arnault, makes this point as follows:

> When a creative team believes in a product, you have to trust the team's gut instinct. That is the case with a new perfume we launched this year: Flower by Kenzo. We put it forward not because of the tests but because the team believed in it. In the tests people did not know what to make if it – the shape of the bottle is different, and its signature flower is a poppy, which has no scent (11).

Key takeouts

1. Insight into consumers is a good catalyst for idea generation, starting with core range extension and then looking at stretch further out.
2. Innovation shortcuts such as competitors, suppliers or other companies can also be used to generate ideas.
3. The process of idea generation is messy and iterative, not tidy and linear, and requires personal passion and tenacity.

Checklist 4: Ideas

	Yes	No
• Do you have a clear idea of market maps and where your brand has areas of underlap?	☐	☐
• Have you started with core range extension ideas before trying bigger stretch?	☐	☐
• Have you gone beyond the consumer altogether and used your own company, the competition and other companies as innovation shortcuts?	☐	☐
• Does your idea-generation plan build in time for several iterations and ways to survive innokill?	☐	☐

 ### Handover

We have seen how insights from consumers, competitors and the company itself can serve as catalysts for generating stretch ideas. We will now look at how to evaluate these ideas and select those with the best potential for building the business and brand. Focusing on doing fewer things but doing them better is critical to avoid the risks of fragmentation.

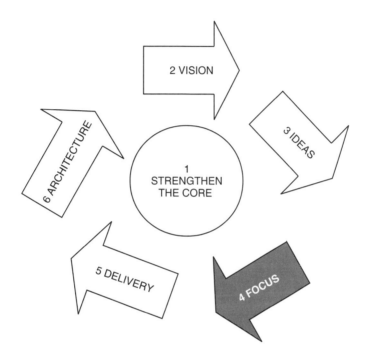

 ## Headlines

Having generated extension ideas, teams need to employ a process to focus on those with the best potential to build the business and the desired brand vision. Clarity is also needed on the company's competences, to ensure that the product promise can be fully delivered. Without such a disciplined approach, companies risk launching too many small extensions that add limited value for consumers and so build little extra business. These extensions also fragment the human and financial resources of a business, leading to value destruction rather than creation.

Meet the seven dwarves

Marketing people love extensions. They provide an opportunity to use all the best bits of the branding toy box, such as concept development, pack design and advertising. However, in many cases extension efforts are wasted on small ideas that add no value for either the consumer or the company. The result is often a classic case of the Pareto principle: 80 per cent of sales are accounted for by 20 per cent of the extensions. Put another way, for every beautiful big idea there are seven dwarves. Human and financial resources are fragmented over too many products or services, leading to a poor return on brand investment.

Launching too many small extensions is one explanation for the woeful state of the UK's National Lottery, rebranded in 2002 as Lotto with a $100 million marketing campaign. This investment and the all-important prize funds were fragmented across an increasingly complex range of extensions such as Lotto Extra, Thunderball and Instants. Despite the heavy marketing support the business actually dropped by more than 5 per cent. As one user commented:

> The problem with The National Lottery is that there are too many brand extensions. It's all too complicated. I think that consumers feel this divides both their attention and the winnings into smaller jackpots. People want one draw and one large jackpot. Everything else complicates the matter and puts people off playing (1).

As with all of marketing, the key to success is focusing on doing fewer things and doing them better. Therefore, a rigorous and disciplined process is needed to review potential extension ideas and assess their potential. The first and most important criterion is ability to build the business. In addition, the potential of the extension to help in building the brand vision should be considered.

Heroes or zeroes?

Combining these two dimensions of business and brand vision building gives an overall assessment of each extension (after all, no business book would be complete without at least one 2 × 2 matrix). For business building, the scale should be in terms of value of sales; profitability should also be noted. The mid-point can be chosen to represent the minimum size of project worth developing and launching. For the brand dimension we are looking not merely for fit with today's image but rather active contribution to building the vision. Four main types of extension fall out of this analysis: hero, cash builder, niche product and drain (Figure 5.1).

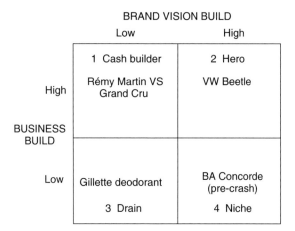

Figure 5.1: Brand and business building matrix.

Hero

These extensions should receive the bulk of the attention and marketing budget for new launches. They generate significant business growth and dramatize the brand vision in a relevant and compelling way. Investment in promoting hero extensions helps improve consumer understanding of the total brand concept, not simply the new product or service. Hero extensions are often 'disruptive', making you sit up, pay attention and change your view of the brand.

The iMac is credited with having changed people's perceptions of Apple, for example. Its revolutionary design was a dramatic visualization of Steve Jobs' vision to get Apple back to what it does best: brilliantly designed products that look great and are user-friendly. The iMac generated pages of free publicity for Apple and sold six million units in the US during its first two years. Other examples include the new Beetle for VW, the Mach 3 razor for Gillette (Figure 5.2) and Levi's Engineered Jeans.

Niche product

This type of extension needs to be handled with extreme care and should be used sparingly. It is small in business terms but is a good dramatization of the desired brand vision. Until it unfortunately fell out of the sky, Concorde played this role for British Airways, having a much bigger image impact than its small passenger numbers would suggest.

However, in many or even most cases these extensions gobble up resources without delivering the expected image-building effects. In the overcrowded world of today's consumers,

Figure 5.2: Hero extension.

many brand messages get lost. Unless an extension is actually bought and used by a consumer, it is unlikely that the new product or service will make a difference to brand perceptions. Therefore, most of the extensions that *do* build brand image are big ideas that are bought by many people, i.e. the hero extensions we saw earlier.

Cash builder

This type of extension has the potential to deliver bags of cash, but is less good at dramatizing the desired brand vision. For many years Rémy Martin cognac refused to compete in the entry level 'VS' market, priding itself on only having products of the superior VSOP grade and above. However, the VS segment was about 30 per cent of the cognac market and so a huge missed opportunity. Finally, Rémy did extend into this segment but with a concept, VS Grand Cru (Figure 5.3), that sought to deliver a higher-quality, more prestigious product and pack, in line with the brand's positioning.

Figure 5.3: Cash builder.

Drain

Drains eat up resources and have a limited impact on either brand image or business growth. The idea of Gillette becoming a 'male grooming' brand offering not merely shavers but also deodorants looked good on paper. However, Gillette failed to convince men that it matched, never mind surpassed, the efficacy of existing brands like Sure and Rexona. Gillette's functional competence was in *shaving* performance and all the deodorants had going for them was the 'sizzle' of masculine, all-American emotional values. Sales and share performance have so far been disappointing, especially given the significant budgets spent on entering this highly competitive market. These funds may have produced a better return if it had been spent on strengthening the core shaving business.

In contrast, Gillette has built a leading 58 per cent share of the £68 million UK shaving cream/gel market in addition to its dominant position in the razor market (78 per cent share). Here, the brand is applying its expertise as a specialist shaving brand to extend into a complementary market (2).

Brand vandal

There is a fifth possible type of extension that in fact has a negative impact on the brand's image. The biggest risk of brand vandalism is launching a poorly performing product, a problem to which we will return in the next chapter on delivery. It can also happen if the extension is *really* out of line with the brand's desired image *and* it achieves high volume.

The cut-priced Porsche 924 is considered to have tarnished the image of the brand in the 1980s, leading to a sharp drop in sales. Owners or potential buyers of the more expensive, authentic 911 sports car were put off by seeing too many cheap 924s driven by middle managers and salespeople (3). However, the more recent Boxster extension seems to have had no such negative impact, despite also having a much lower price. It seems to have better captured 'Porscheness' in its styling and performance.

Even more controversial for Porsche is its imminent entry into the 4 × 4 sports utility vehicle market with the Cayenne (Figure 5.4). Some observers are understandably concerned

Figure 5.4: Porsche Cayenne – brand builder or brand vandal?

about this move, which does feel like a big stretch. Nevertheless, press reviews have been positive and the company has sold out its first 18 months' supply before the launch. Time will tell, but perhaps the Cayenne is far enough away from the core for 911 drivers to be able to accept it without too much of a problem.

We will now look at a practical example of applying the brand and business building matrix, before reviewing in more detail each of these two dimensions.

Bertolli: Virtual venture capital

In many cases brand teams have no shortage of possible extension ideas. The real issue is the one faced by Bertolli in the Netherlands during 2002: which ones to focus on? The Italian food brand had no less than 30 possible extensions, far too many to progress. The team needed to select which horses to back and designed an 'innovation roadmap' showing the launch sequencing.

Strong foundations for growth

The good news was that a great job had been done on the first two steps of the Brand Stretch workout. First, there was a strong and healthy core product in olive oil, which had taken a leading position in the Dutch market. This symbolized all the positive associations of Italy, both functionally (natural, tasty, healthy) and emotionally (sunshine, good times with friends and family). Second, a big masterbrand idea had been developed as an umbrella concept for a broader product range. The promise was all about 'giving people a true taste of Italian pleasure', underpinned by the benefit of 'truly tasty Italian food that is easy to prepare and enjoy'. The brand truth of having genuine 'olive oil inside' was a real edge versus other 'fake' Italian food brands such as Dolmio.

Elevator pitching

A key challenge was how to review the 30 or so extension proposals in a few hours, not several days. The solution was to think like a 'virtual venture capital company'. The team members were asked to imagine that they had a limited amount of capital to invest in new extensions. Prospective 'project entrepreneurs' would then 'pitch' their ideas to try to secure backing. Rather than the usual 20 pages of PowerPoint slides, each project leader completed a simple one-page 'New ventures proposal' (Table 5.1). This asked probing questions about the estimated business build. It also helped assess how good the idea was at bringing to life

Table 5.1: Example of new ventures proposal.

New Ventures Proposal

WHAT: What is the extension idea? Product? Packaging? Price point?

. . . .
. . . .

WHY: Why will people want to buy it?

. . . .
. . . .

WHERE: Where will people buy it?

. . . .

WHEN: *Earliest* possible launch date . . . .
           Recommended launch date . . . .

BRINGING TO LIFE THE VISION:

	LOW	OK	HIGH
• Value driver 1:	☐	☐	☐
• Value driver 2:	☐	☐	☐
• Value driver 3:	☐	☐	☐
• Value driver 4:	☐	☐	☐
• Value driver 5:	☐	☐	☐
OVERALL BRAND-NESS	Low	OK	High

BUSINESS POTENTIAL:

• Consumer appeal:	Low	OK	High
• Differentiation:	Low	OK	High
• Sales million euros (5 yrs):	Low	OK	High
• Gross profit margin %:	☐		
OVERALL BUSINESS POTENTIAL:	Low	OK	High

the Bertolli vision, in particular the key value drivers such as 'freshness', 'Italian-ness' and 'taste enjoyment'. This approach forced people to make short and snappy presentations and also made it much easier to compare the different proposals.

Place your bets

A huge wall chart was used to map the ideas on the brand and business-building dimensions (Figure 5.5). A good amount of healthy debate ensued about where different extensions sat, with project leaders passionately making their case. To arrive at the final shortlist of six or seven ideas, the team members were asked to 'place their bets' by allocating an imaginary $10 million of venture capital to no more than three ideas. The following examples illustrate outputs from the brand and business matrix (extension candidates have been changed for confidentiality reasons).

Hero: Olive oil

This product still has potential to drive sales growth as the market is growing due to more people starting to use olive oil. Also it is *the* perfect symbolization of the masterbrand concept and the core product truth for other items in the range.

Cash builder: Spread

The spread delivers a significant new revenue stream for the brand and also gets the brand into many more homes, as it competes in a huge market. It is less strong on image building,

Figure 5.5: Bertolli brand and business building matrix.

being a manufactured product that is not typically Italian. However, the olive oil ingredient makes it *more* natural than your average margarine and it is also strong on the benefit of vitality. In addition, brilliant advertising brings to life the Bertolli world by communicating positive health and well-being in a highly entertaining fashion. It shows Italians enjoying life at a ripe old age thanks to their olive-oil-rich diet. The tongue-in-cheek tagline 'Club 18–130' sums up the benefit of 'enjoyable longevity'.

Niche product: Balsamico vinegar

This has very strong values of authentic Italian-ness, and is also a complementary ingredient to olive oil for making salad dressings. Given the small sales, the product is given little or no support, surviving on point-of-sale promotion, PR and the halo effect of other brand support.

Drain: Mayonnaise

This is not a great image builder, being a traditional Dutch product that you have with french fries rather than one you expect to see on an Italian's table. Also, unlike the spread, the product and pack lack any real added value versus the competition and as a result mayonnaise is small in sales terms. Support is being reduced and it may eventually be delisted.

Roadmap

Building the innovation roadmap took into account practical issues, such as the earliest possible launch date. The number of launches per year was limited to two or three, to ensure each got the right support. The team also tried to sequence the product launches in such a way that Bertolli gradually built its credibility as a true food brand. The first stage of going from a mono-product to a specialist brand had been achieved with direct stretch into spreads and other olive-oil-based products such as pesto. The next stage was to create an umbrella concept that supported a wider range of products that added food values and taste enjoyment to the brand, such as pasta sauces. The final stage was to offer complete meal solutions such as ready meals, already being successfully test marketed in the USA.

We will look in more detail at how to establish the business and brand building potential of an extension. (If you feel you have the knack of this already, feel free to skip the next few pages.)

Dimension one: Brand vision building

The theory here is that extensions don't simply borrow awareness and reputation from the masterbrand that launches them. They are also supposed to feed back positive values, a little like someone paying back a loan from the bank with interest. Many marketing consultants like to draw a nice neat 'virtuous circle' of feedback to illustrate this model. However, lazy or incorrect use of this model means that very few extensions have the promised image-building effects.

The first problem is summed up by the attitude of a brand ego tripper in a top marketing company: 'The main objective of extending a brand is to build the brand's equity. Any increase in sales is a bonus.' Frightening stuff. This mindset leads to launches that fit the brand's image needs but not those of consumers. These extensions end up being dwarf ideas that in reality make little impact on the bottom line or the brand image (Figure 5.6).

The second mistake is to ignore how the extension *reinforces* the existing masterbrand promise that made you famous in the first place and only consider what it is adding. The most popular chart is one showing how the extension will 'borrow authenticity and heritage' and 'feed back modernity and innovation'. To avoid this sloppy strategy, you need to consider not one but three key questions about any extension, as shown in Table 5.2.

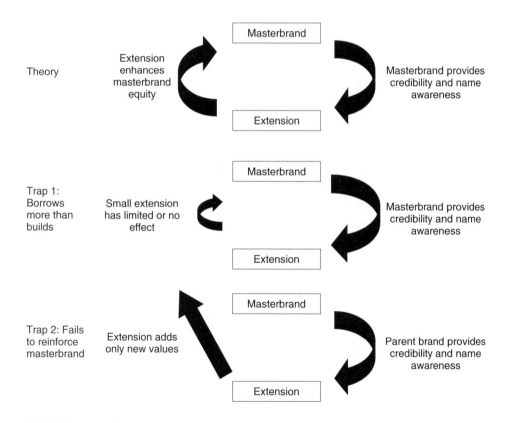

Figure 5.6: Virtuous circle traps.

Table 5.2: Image impact questions.

1. **Reinforce:** how will it reinforce the current strengths in the brand promise?	2. **Add:** which positive new values and benefits will it add?	3. **Subtract:** are there any aspects that are inconsistent with the brand vision?
⋮	⋮	⋮

Innovation stimulation

Extensions may have some positive effects on the masterbrand *image* and enhance the ability to launch future extensions. However, unless something fundamental is done to improve the core product range, no pick-up in *sales* is likely. Take the launch of the striking PT Cruiser by Chrysler (Figure 5.7). As one observer noted:

> So far, there is little indication that the craze over the PT is sparking enthusiasm in the U.S. for other Chrysler-brand vehicles (4).

On the other hand, what hero extensions *can* do is stimulate and inspire a renewed product offering in terms of the core product, packaging and communication.

Figure 5.7: Chrysler PT Cruiser.

Reproduced by permission of DaimlerChrysler UK Ltd.

Product and packaging

The iMac was not a one-hit wonder with which Apple got lucky. It inspired a stream of new extensions that reinvented the core product range (Figure 5.8). The brand had always stood for innovation and ease of use, but lost its way in the early 1990s trying to play catch-up with the PC makers. iMac was the start of the revival of the brand and business when the company refocused on what it stood for, what made it different from the competition. It stopped making beige boxes like every other brand and started doing what it was best at, pushing the boundaries forward with innovative, appealing and relevant products.

Communication

Communication for Bacardi rum in the mid-1990s had a hard, rough and masculine edge. It featured boxers from the brand's home country of Cuba fighting it out in the 1950s. A rethink was prompted by the success of the Bacardi Breezer extension's lighthearted 'Latin spirit in everyone' campaign. This showed how there is Latin attitude and behaviour hiding inside even the most conservative of Brits. The team concluded that Bacardi was after all a party brand and much less serious than other white spirits like vodka. This inspired a new campaign for the core rum that emphasized fun, energy and enjoyment while keeping the brand's Latin roots to the forefront. The campaign, called 'Welcome to the Latin Quarter', has been successful in maintaining the core rum business, despite the huge push behind Breezer.

Dimension two: Show me the money

The most important question to ask about the potential extension is the size of business growth it will deliver. There are many ways of evaluating business building potential. One simple approach asks four questions about the extension (Figure 5.9). These may seem basic and straightforward, but the overcrowded extension graveyard suggests that they are all too often ignored. The first two questions concern concept appeal and the final two concern the company itself:

- Is it compelling?
- Is it credible?
- Do we have the competence needed?
- Is the extension complementary to the existing range?

Don't you want me baby? (Compelling)

The most important question for an extension is how compelling the concept is. In many cases, extensions offer new features but these fail to deliver a relevant benefit. For example,

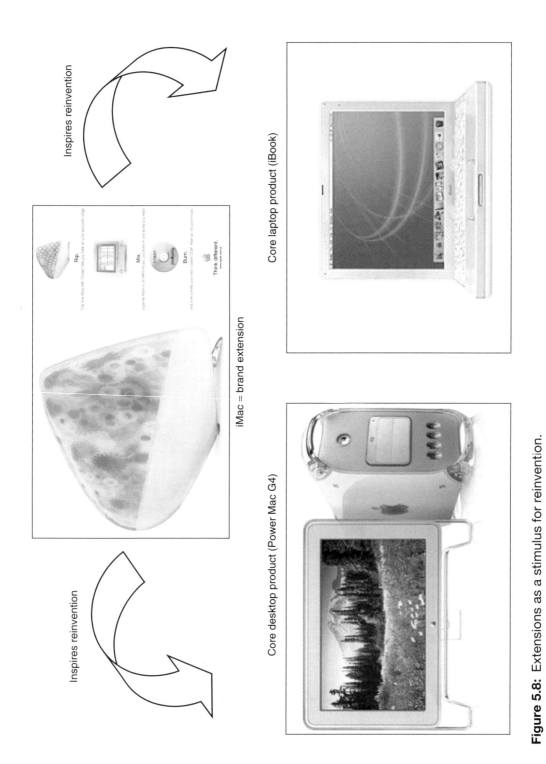

Inspires reinvention

iMac = brand extension

Inspires reinvention

Core laptop product (iBook)

Core desktop product (Power Mac G4)

Figure 5.8: Extensions as a stimulus for reinvention.

Images courtesy of Apple.

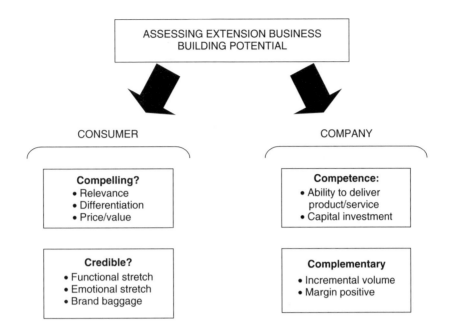

Figure 5.9: Assessing the business building potential of extensions.

ice beer never really took off. Lager beers were already served cold and delivered refreshment, so the claimed extra refreshment of ice beer was not relevant. There are several factors to consider when evaluating the relevance of an extension.

Is it solving a problem. . .

For example, Nurofen Meltlets melt in the mouth when you need pain relief but don't have access to water. In contrast, Ariel Hygiene washing powder's promise to remove germs from clothes through anti-bacterial action was not relevant to consumers, and the extension was killed.

. . .or making life a little better?

Häagen-Dazs stretched from tubs of ice cream into small pots and ice creams on sticks (Figure 5.10). These extensions delivered a new level of pleasure and indulgence to the 'impulse' out-of-home ice-cream market.

Is it different?

To have a chance of creating sustainable growth, the extension needs some degree of differentiation. This is partly to do with the tangible product or service concept itself. The

Figure 5.10: A compelling extension – making life a little better.

Reproduced by permission of The Pillsbury Company.

intangible imagery of the brand adds another more emotional dimension of differentiation. In the case of the iMac, the product itself was unique in its design and ease of use. The addition of the Apple name added addition values of creativity and imagination that are very different to those of IBM or Dell.

Value for money

Many extensions fail by offering poor value for money. Getting the price point right is often key to generating trial by minimizing the 'price risk' a consumer has to take to try the new idea. It also ensures that the extension is integrated into everyday usage habits. However, brand teams often overestimate how much people are prepared to pay for the benefits they are bringing to the market. The extension of Unilever's Persil washing powder into home laundry services with My Home had great appeal for today's time-starved, busy world. It offered to pick up your laundry, wash and iron it and bring it back. However, the high price per item put people off, leading to limited trial and the sale of the business.

Market attractiveness

The attractiveness of the new market is another key issue to consider when evaluating the extension's potential. The most basic factors are market size, market growth and intensity of competition. A further question to consider when assessing market potential is whether you are going against or with the flow of consumer habits:

- *Against the tide*: trying to change a consumer habit is a long hard slog and tends to limit extension potential without huge investment. The Comfort brand of fabric softener had the neat idea of offering a portable, handbag-friendly spray called Refresh for removing bad odours on clothes. Initial trial was good, but occasional usage meant that few people ever bought a second bottle.
- *With the tide*: extensions that build on an existing habit tend to be bigger. Comfort had much more success with the launch of Comfort Vaporesse, which fragrances clothes when

used instead of water in a steam iron. Here, consumers are not adding an action, but rather replacing one with another. In addition, ironing is an everyday habit, so the number of possible usage occasions is high.

Trust me, I'm a brand (Credible)

Credibility depends on the stretch between current perceptions of the brand and the extension. The further the stretch, the more investment will be needed to overcome consumers' doubts and achieve trial. Big stretch *is* possible, but the level and duration of support needed may make a new brand a better alternative. Not one but two dimensions need to be considered: functional and emotional. Taken together, these help highlight the boundaries of brand stretch and guide the optimum branding approach (Figure 5.11).

Functional stretch

This dimension concerns the credibility of the brand's delivering the functional benefits in the concept. For example, Special K built a reputation for tasty, nutritious breakfast cereals

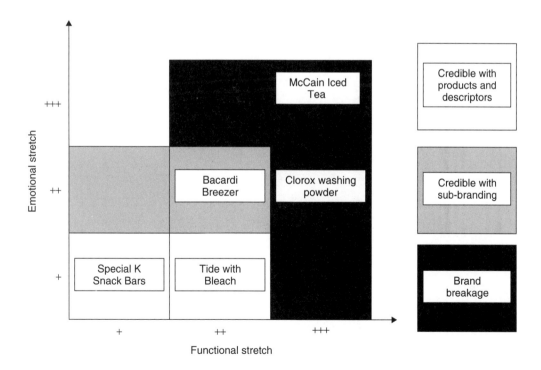

Figure 5.11: Brand credibility boundaries.

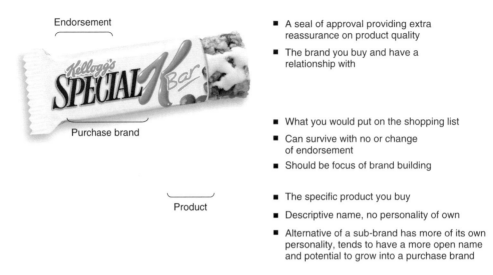

Endorsement

- A seal of approval providing extra reassurance on product quality
- The brand you buy and have a relationship with

Purchase brand

- What you would put on the shopping list
- Can survive with no or change of endorsement
- Should be focus of brand building

Product

- The specific product you buy
- Descriptive name, no personality of own
- Alternative of a sub-brand has more of its own personality, tends to have a more open name and potential to grow into a purchase brand

Figure 5.12: Branding hierarchy for functional stretch.

Reproduced by permission of The Kellogg Company.

for people watching their figures. It was a relatively small functional stretch for the brand to offer a cereal bar (Figure 5.12). This met a real need by being tasty but having the same calories as only three potato chips. The bar has added an incremental $20 million to the brand's sales in the UK.

With purely functional stretch like this, there is no need for a change in brand personality and tone, leading to a branding solution as follows:

- The *purchase brand* that people bought and had a relationship with could stay the same.
- A simple *descriptor* name was used to introduce the new product.
- Kellogg's provided additional *endorsement* on quality and reliability.

Sometimes *ownable descriptors* are used to give a twist that makes a version's name a little more distinctive. Absolut has done this with its flavoured vodkas (see Figure 5.13), such as Absolut Citron (rather than lemon) and Absolut Kurant (rather than blackcurrant).

In contrast, the extension of the US bleach brand Clorox into washing powder in 1988 failed to convince consumers of its functional credibility. It was weighed down by negative brand baggage: concerns about it being harsh and lacking clothes care expertise. Despite $225 million of development and marketing support, the extension achieved only a 3 per cent share. An extension of the leading washing powder, Tide with Bleach, had much more success, achieving a 17 per cent share despite being second to market. The functional stretch for Tide was much smaller, given the brand's expertise in clothes washing and care (5).

Figure 5.13: Ownable descriptors.

Emotional stretch

Emotional stretch occurs when the personality, tone and style of the extension are different to those of the masterbrand. As with people, this is more difficult than changing jobs (i.e. functional stretch). A *sub-brand* allows more emotional stretch than a simple descriptor (e.g. Bacardi Breezer versus Bacardi Lime and Soda). Here, the extension starts to break out of the masterbrand's universe and take on more of its own personality. Like a son or daughter, the sub-brand shares the same family values and name, but has a life of its own. Launching a totally new brand, possibly with some low-key *endorsement*, gives even more stretch but less leverage of the masterbrand (Figure 5.14).

Sub-branding to allow more emotional stretch may be needed for several reasons:

- *New target audience*: such as the launch of the Martini V2 pre-mix for younger people.
- *Going up the value curve*: as with the more aspirational, higher-quality Gold Blend coffee from Nescafé, which offered real added value in product (ground versus granules) and packaging (unique shape).

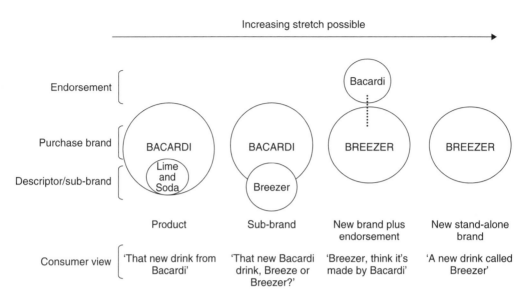

Figure 5.14: Branding options for different levels of stretch.

- *Going down the value curve*: such as Kodak Funtime film, ensuring that the product does feel and look like it is offering 'less for less', not the same product at a lower price.

Going down the value curve is especially risky, as it can undermine the parent brand's image among current users and encourage them to 'trade down'. This is especially harmful where prestige and exclusivity are part of the brand concept. One study showed that a down-market extension of BMW had a negative impact on brand image among users, although this was reduced by the use of a sub-brand (6). Levi's obviously thinks that it can get away with a move down market through its Signature range of cheap jeans for Wal-Mart and other discount supermarkets. However, even with a sub-brand this seems a dangerous move for a brand where 'image is everything'. Gap tried a similar move with Gap Warehouse, but eventually replaced this with the Old Navy brand.

Brand breakage

There are limits to how far a brand can be *profitably* stretched, even with sub-branding. Take McCain's brand ego trip from french fries into iced tea, with the McCain Colorado sub-brand. It had delusions of being an American lifestyle brand that offered all the foods that went with this. In reality, McCain sold frozen convenience food in supermarkets and lacked the emotional credibility to compete effectively in the soft drinks market. In addition, there was a functional question about the taste of an iced tea made by a frozen spud seller.

McCain has now wisely dropped the iced tea in most markets to refocus on its core range of potato-based products. In addition, it has stretched into the adjacent markets of frozen and microwaveable pizzas.

Where the stretch is very far, developing a new brand may produce a better return on investment. The Prudential took this route when launching an online bank in 1998. It was concerned that the fresh, vibrant and funky personality needed to compete in this new market was a million miles away from the reliable but dusty image of the Pru. This led to the creation of the egg brand, which has gone on to be one of the very few dot-com brands that has not become a dot-bomb. It has now moved into profit and counts over two million customers on its books.

Bringing home some *new* bacon (Complementary)

The extension should ideally complement the existing product range in order to maximize the incremental profit generated. The two issues to consider are how much of the volume is incremental and the profitability of the extension itself, issues that were discussed earlier in Chapter 2.

Source of business

Incremental volume and profit growth for the business as a whole are ultimately what matters with an extension. Therefore, assessing the degree of cannibalization of existing products is key. This risk is highest with core range extensions, especially those that are not sufficiently new and different.

Extension profitability

Brand extensions should be an opportunity to improve profitability by launching added-value products and services that support a price premium. A trap to avoid is offering a 'plus' that increases the cost of goods but not pricing up in line with this. Inability to support a price premium should force you to consider whether the additional benefits are adding value for the consumer or merely complexity.

Can we make it? (Company competence)

A lack of company competence and expertise may make it hard to deliver against the promises made in the concept without significant capital investment. Even if the brand can stretch conceptually, the company may find it hard to deliver a sufficient return on capital. For example, the stretch of Mars from confectionery into ice cream is a textbook classic.

Talk to insiders, however, and they say that the company is yet to make much money out of this venture, even after a decade of heavy investment. This brave move involved major capital costs to build new factories and for many years capacity utilization was too low to generate a good return on capital.

Stretching product brands into the service sector is one area where the lack of competence has tripped companies up. The theory is that these ventures are brilliant image builders, creating a universe where the brand concept comes to life. The harsh reality is that they are businesses just like any other. Unless plenty of punters are pulled in, the 'To let' sign will be up before you know it, as was the case with Lynx barbershops and the Capital Radio Café. Consumer goods companies have learnt the hard way that service businesses need a different skills set and also big investment to attain scale if they are to be profitable.

The easyGroup is an example of a brand that has discovered the risks of not understanding and leveraging its core competences.

The easyGroup story: Murder on the balance sheet

Stelios Haji-Ioannou, the charismatic chairman of easyGroup, is giving his role model Richard Branson a real run for his money in the brand ego tripping stakes. As one article said, 'The new chicks have yet to fly the nest and remain reliant on their parent – for money as well as management.' According to this article, the internet café, credit card and online shopping comparison service extensions have two main things in common. First, they have submerged most of the money made by easyJet (over $100 million in 2002) in a sea of red ink. The internet café business alone has so far lost (are you sitting down?) $150 million. Expansion was too fast, with 20 cafés opened in eight different countries before the business model was proven. The shopping comparison service is a virtual business in every sense, with few customers and losses of $7 million. The credit card has all of 1500 customers and losses of $4 million (Figure 5.15) (7).

The second common point of most of these extensions is that they seem to have little to do with the core competences developed in the core easyJet business. easyGroup does claim to have learnt from these mistakes and plans to refocus on extensions where it can leverage the following competences:

- *No frills*: there must be an opportunity to remove frills that are seen by a large group of consumers as non-essential, such as food and drinks on airlines (Figure 5.16). There were fewer frills to remove in credit cards and online shopping. Removing frills means that costs can be cut out and some of these savings passed on to the consumer in lower prices.
- *Price elasticity*: offering lower prices should not merely steal market share, it should bring in new consumers who would not normally have purchased. This is something that easyJet

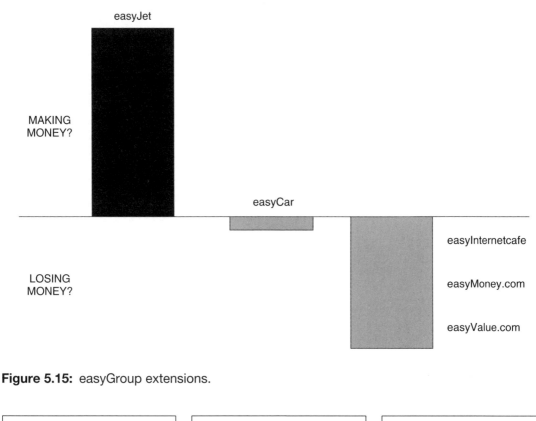

Figure 5.15: easyGroup extensions.

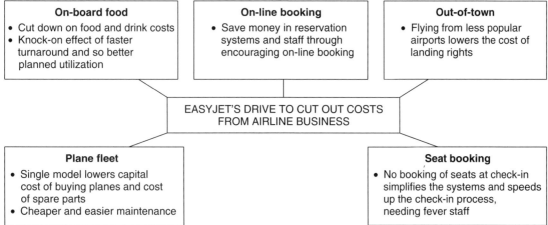

Figure 5.16: easyJet's stripping out of costs.

and other low-cost airlines have done well, growing the market for air travel. The problem with the credit card business here is that offering really low rates attracted customers with a poor credit record, screwing up the business model.

- *Yield management*: easyGroup has a real competence in 'sweating' physical assets through improving their utilization. With easyJet it has developed models and systems to manage prices over time to fill up the planes. Book early and you pay less, book at the last minute and you pay for the privilege. This technique also allows easyGroup to advertise incredibly low, attention-grabbing prices in its advertising (although there are the beginnings of discontent about what you have to do to get these prices).
- *Consumer outsourcing*: there must be opportunities to get consumers to do some or most of the work, such as online booking of flights and fighting for a seat rather than having one pre-assigned. This cuts down staff costs to a minimum, and also helps ensure a better consistency of service.

The car rental company easyCar has a fighting chance of breaking even in 2003, reflecting a good fit with these competences (Figure 5.17). There are frills to remove, such as a wide choice of cars. Price elasticity means that lower prices bring in new users: 77 per cent of easyCar customers had not considered another hire car firm. Consumer outsourcing includes getting you to wash your own hire car or pay £10 to have it cleaned when you return the vehicle. This came from observing that much of the time in a conventional hire car business was spent cleaning and washing. About 80–90 per cent of easyCar consumers return the car clean, saving on staff costs but also reducing turnaround time and so improving load factors. And easyCar plans to go one step further by allowing you to pick up a car from a staffless

	easyCar	easyCinema
▪ Removing frills	** (Model choice)	0 (Popcorn plus...?)
▪ Outsource to consumer	*** (Book on-line, wash car yourself, pick up yourself in future)	0 (Book on-line plus...?)
▪ Cut prices/elastic prices	*** (Big opportunity to cut price and attract new category users)	* Less opportunity to cut price? Off-peak prices already offered
▪ Yield management	*** (Book early and pay less is attractive)	* Spontaneous decision for many people?
OVERALL FIT	***	0/*?

Figure 5.17: easyGroup extensions and competence fit.

location. The car is unlocked remotely when a trusted easyCar customer calls through on their mobile phone.

Also on the cards are easyDorm hotels. Here, there is a model to copy in the French Formulae One hotel chain. You check in with your credit card, bring your own booze, forget about room service, but get away with change from $30 for one night's stay. Equally, easyJet itself was a carbon copy of the highly successful US business Southwest Airlines.

There are signs that Stelios is far from ready to quit his brand ego trip; as he admits himself, he is having too much fun. The latest venture, easyCinema, seems a poor fit with the group's competences. As one observer joked, 'Apart from the popcorn, what other frills will be removed? Perhaps the seats and the films!' And I am yet to find anyone who is interested in advance, low-price booking with easyPizza.

> **easyGroup summary**
>
> 1. Be clear on your competences.
> 2. Focus on using these competences to add value in new markets.
> 3. Avoid brand ego trips that stray from these competences, unless you have rich parents.

Alternatives to going it alone

Licensing

Brand licensing involves giving another company the rights to use the brand name and associated symbols and imagery in return for a fee. This fee is typically 10–12 per cent of the sales revenues generated, but can vary widely. In the past, licensing has mainly been used by lifestyle brands, such as Disney in entertainment and Ralph Lauren in fashion. Disney used licensing to create a completely new, multibillion-dollar business called Disney Consumer Products off the back of blockbuster animated movies such as *The Lion King*. Increasingly, less glamorous consumer goods businesses are also jumping on the licensing bandwagon. You can now buy Cadbury's chocolate desserts and M&Ms-flavoured ice cream thanks to licensing deals done by the companies owning these brands.

Upsides

The *main attractions* of brand licensing are threefold. First, you generate a new profit stream with no capital investment, so greatly enhancing the firm's return on capital. Second, the launch itself has more chance of success as you are tapping into real sector expertise, such as Pespi's distribution of Starbucks' Frappuccino in grocery stores. Finally, the licensed product helps generate awareness for the brand that should in theory rub off on the core products.

Downsides

As always, there are also *downsides* to be managed. First, careful quality control is needed to ensure that the licensed products deliver the required quality. There should be some 'brand added value' beyond what Disney calls 'logo slapping', simply applying the brand logo to a mediocre product. It was not obvious how the *Cosmopolitan* magazine brand was going to add value to yoghurts, and these did not last long. In contrast, other licensed ventures into sex guides and bedclothes fit better with the brand's desired personality of being glamorous, fun, modern and sexy (Figure 5.18).

In addition, the amount of valuable management time spent on licensed products needs to be controlled. This is because in many cases licensed products make great classroom case studies but generate peanuts for profits. Few brands can match the image appeal and badge value of Harley-Davidson. Yet even this company only generates about $5 million in fees from its international licensing (don't be fooled by the reported retail sales of $150 million:

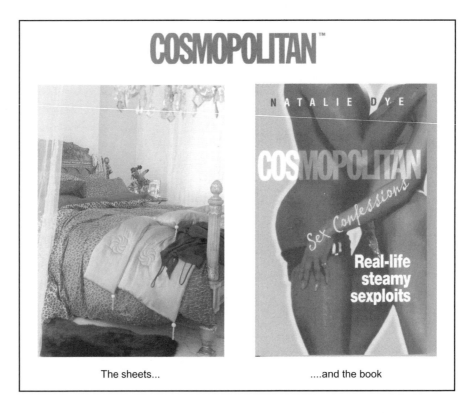

Figure 5.18: *Cosmopolitan* licensed products.

halve this to get to wholesale price, then multiply that by the 10 per cent licensing fee to get to the real money). Also, it is hard to see the image-building benefits of a wine cooler (now killed) and a L'Oréal perfume (still sold in France and Germany) for a brand that sells big bikes to blokes with an average age of 46 (8).

Co-branding

Co-branding is another alternative to going it alone with extensions. It involves two companies combining brands on a single product to enhance appeal and differentiation. A primary brand is complemented with a secondary brand that provides additional credibility or appeal. Orbit chewing gum (primary) has enhanced its dental protection capacity with the addition of the Crest brand (secondary). In this case, the co-branding is more than merely adding a logo; P&G is also providing dental care technology.

Key takeouts

1. Poor use of brand extension can end up fragmenting a business rather than strengthening it.
2. Human and financial resources should be focused on those extensions that have real potential to build both business and the brand vision.
3. The competences of a company are also a key consideration that may limit brand stretch. Licensing the brand to another company that has the required expertise may be a better way to maximize return on investment.

Checklist 5: Focus

	Yes	No
• What is the evidence that the extension is meeting a relevant consumer need?	☐	☐
• Is the extension truly differentiated versus the core product and competition?	☐	☐
• Is the functional and emotional stretch from the core brand credible?	☐	☐
• Is the extension helping reinforce the core masterbrand concept, not just trying to add new benefits?	☐	☐
• Are you sure you have the competence to make a product or service that delivers better than the competition?	☐	☐

 **Handover**

We have seen how to focus resources on the extension ideas with the biggest potential for brand and business building. We will now go on to look at the important but often overlooked issues of execution. The next chapter on delivery will highlight the need to build multiple levels of differentiation into your product or service to avoid the mistake of overpromising.

Step Five: Delivery

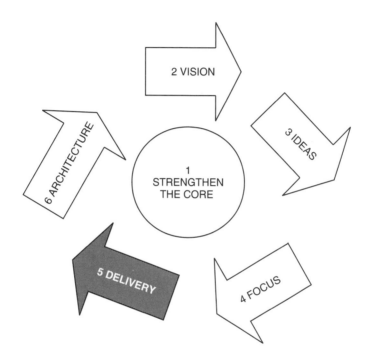

 ## Headlines

Even when you have focused your efforts and investment on the extensions with the best potential, poor execution can let you down. Failing to deliver on the promises made in the concept is rated by marketing directors as one of the main causes of extension failure. In contrast, excellence of execution has several positive effects. First and foremost, it helps boost repurchase and so increases the probability of profitable growth. It also helps generate positive word of mouth and free publicity, by far the best forms of extension promotion. Finally, product quality can allow you to push the brand stretch boundaries: people will tend to buy a fantastic product, even if the fit with the brand is not obvious.

Underestimating execution

Brand ego trippers focus on theory not action. They think that strategy is *the* key to success, when it is at most half the answer. Take debates about the extension of Persil from washing powder into dishwashing liquid, as recalled by one ex-Unilever marketing director:

> The brand teams spent days locked in discussions about how far the equity of Persil could stretch and what impact the new launch would have on the 'mother brand' image. However, the most fundamental issue that was often overlooked was whether we could develop a better washing-up liquid than the market leader Fairy.

In reality, execution is just as important as strategy in determining the success of a brand extension. Marketing directors put failure to deliver against the promise at the top of their list of reasons for unsuccessful extensions (Figure 6.1). They rate this factor as twice as important as the often quoted reason of poor brand fit. Nescafé Hot When You Want is a good example of a brand extension that overpromised, underdelivered and paid the price.

Nescafé Hot When You Want: Not so hot execution

The extension was a perfectly good idea. It made coffee accessible to people on the move via an innovative self-heating can (Figure 6.2). The packaging format was closer to the codes of soft drinks, adding modernity and hopefully youth appeal. A test in 5000 stores was started with $3.75 million of above-the-line marketing support, including a television campaign. However, the can failed to heat up the coffee fully, especially in the colder months of the UK winter. As the marketing director for impulse drinks wryly commented, 'We had some

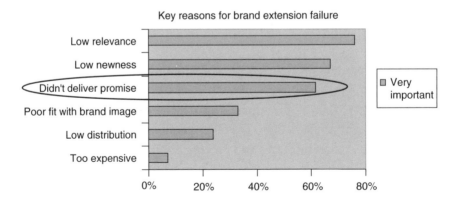

Figure 6.1: Failure factors for brand extensions.

Source: brandgym research with marketing directors.

Figure 6.2: Nescafé Hot When You Want.

Reproduced by permission of Nestlé UK Ltd.

consumers referring to it as "Warm when you want" (1). Other flaws in the execution banged further nails in the coffin. The quantity of liquid inside the can was much smaller than the size of pack suggested, creating a poor impression of value for money. Unclear variant differentiation meant that people often picked up the one with sugar rather than without, or vice versa. Penetration reached 15 per cent after five months, but tailed off when people failed to buy the product again. The plug was pulled and the Nescafé team went back to the drawing board.

Brand damage

Delivering a poor product experience is not only bad for the extension. It can also make people re-evaluate their opinions of other products in the range that they already use, as shown by a brandgym study with UK consumers. A whacking 86 per cent of consumers said that they would feel more negative about other products in the range after trying a poorly

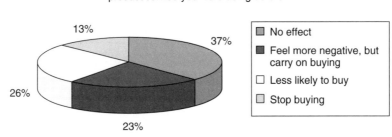

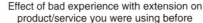

Effect of bad experience with extension on
product/service you were using before

Figure 6.3: Effect of poor extensions on other products in range.

Source: The brandgym, April 2003.

performing extension. Even more of a concern is the 39 per cent who would go as far as re-evaluating their purchase of these products (Figure 6.3).

The closer an extension is to the core of the brand, the bigger the risk of undermining consumer confidence in the masterbrand promise. In extreme circumstances the effects can be catastrophic, as with the Audi 5000's 'sudden acceleration' problem that resulted in fatal accidents. Brand sales imploded, falling from 74 000 in 1985 to 21 000. The Audi 5000 was of course the worst affected, but adverse publicity had a damaging 'spill-over' effect on other models (2).

When the stretch is further away, the negative consequences are less severe. For example, the appalling service record of Virgin trains may make you think twice about flying Virgin Atlantic, as the two travel businesses are closely related. However, it is less likely to stop you using Virgin Telecom or Virgin Finance.

Bouncing back

One of the major benefits of a strong brand is its ability to recover from a life-threatening extension, such as the phoenix-like performance of the UK's leading laundry detergent, Persil. The ill-fated Persil Power extension in 1994 was supposed to be Unilever's ultimate weapon in the fight against arch-rival Procter & Gamble. However, Procter was quick to jump on rumours that the manganese-based 'accelerator' in the new Persil product could rot clothes under certain washing conditions. Television presenters were soon holding up pants full of Persil Power-induced holes on the evening news. In the three months following the launch shares dropped from 27.4 to 24.2 per cent, a $45 million hole in retail sales. However, within a couple of years the brand had clawed back the share losses, and in 2003 it was a healthy market leader again with a share of almost 30 per cent (3).

Brand and deliver

The good news is that delivering against your promises pays off. Most importantly, this generates better levels of repurchase and loyalty. It also creates positive word of mouth, which is invaluable in boosting trial. The brandgym stretch study quoted earlier shows that over 70 per cent of consumers that have a *good* product experience feel more positive about other products in a brand's range. Almost half of people would be more likely to try other products in the range as a result (Figure 6.4).

One company that seems to be crystal clear about the importance of product quality in protecting brand integrity is BMW, as described by Chris Bangle, global chief of design:

> I often appeal to a deeply held, almost nonverbal sense about BMW-ness. A certain pride of product shared by everyone in the company that expresses itself in the classic quality of our cars, from the purring engines to the buttery seats. Every employee here knows that if a car doesn't have these things, it's simply not a BMW – and customers won't buy it (4).

One example of an extension that has delivered extensively against its promises is the Apple iPod MP3 music player.

The Apple iPod: White hot execution

The Apple iPod MP3 music player has been the first major success of Apple outside its core area of computer-related products. It illustrates beautifully how fantastic execution can help a brand stretch into new markets. Sales were estimated at as many as half a million for the final quarter of 2002, giving Apple a forecast 15 per cent share of the global MP3 player market (5).

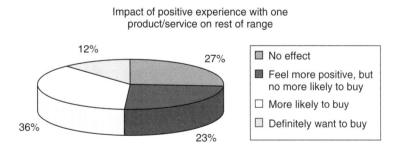

Figure 6.4: Effect of good experience on other products in range.

Source: The brandgym, April 2003.

The iPod is one of the most accomplished designs of the Apple Design Group, led by Jonathan Ive. It truly has a 'wow' factor about it. With a white Perspex-covered face and chrome back, it looks sleek, cool and like no other MP3 player. It successfully draws on the design roots of the titanium Apple G4 PowerBook and the all-white iBook. Point-of-sale promotion ensured that shoppers could see the product in all its glory, by encasing the iPod in Perspex, with the face accessible so that you could try it out. Importantly, the design excellence has been applied in the whole package, not just the product. A beautiful white box houses the iPod and spare ear plug covers come in vacuum-sealed plastic that looks more like Prada cosmetic packaging than that of an electronic product (Figure 6.5).

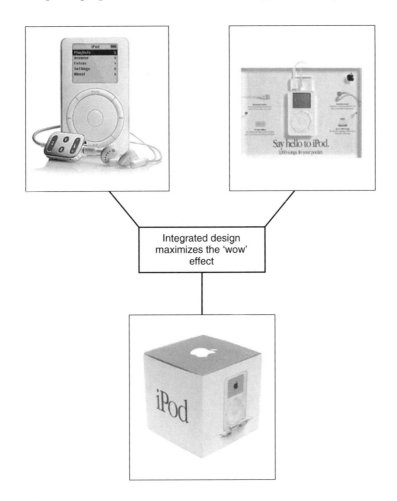

Figure 6.5: Total design of the Apple iPod.

Images courtesy of Apple.

Not only does the iPod look amazing, it has performance that blows away the competition. It can store between 2000 and 4000 tracks depending on the model bought; many MP3 players have 5 per cent or less of this storage capacity. And all this in a player the size of a cigarette case! In addition, the connection to the PC uses a different technology to that of most MP3 players (Firewire instead of USB). This means that you can download an album from your PC in seconds rather than minutes. (In case you are wondering, I have not been paid by Apple to spout so enthusiastically about its product, it genuinely is that good.)

The iPod's success also demonstrates the value of a fantastic product in generating free publicity. The design and performance of the product meant that happy users became product fans who told and showed *everyone* about their new purchase. In addition, this buzz was boosted by unanimously positive press coverage that recognized the breakthrough nature of Apple's innovation. Despite limited advertising investment, the product received good levels of awareness and interest.

The incredible success of the iPod makes you wonder about where Apple could go next. After years of fighting the 'Wintel' (Windows and Intel) army of PCs in a battle that is seemingly impossible to win, perhaps it should look to brand stretch as a better bet? Surely the breakthrough design of the iPod could be used to inspire a range of other personal electronic products, such as portable phones and personal organizers?

> ### Apple iPod summary
>
> 1. 'It's about the product, stupid.'
> 2. Hot products create buzz worth its weight in gold.
> 3. Think about the total design concept, including point of sale and outer packaging.

We will now look in more detail at how product, packaging and distribution can help you deliver against your extension promises. (If the iPod story has given you enough ideas on this already, skip to the next chapter.)

Delivering the promise

Delivering your promise is about not merely *thinking* different, but also *doing* different. Wherever possible, the best solution is to build several layers of differentiation. This is especially true today when the speed of competitive response is so fast, leaving you a limited window of opportunity to exploit an idea. Building multiple dimensions of differentiation makes it much harder for competitors to copy the brand extension, as they have to replicate many different elements.

The product dimension

Behind many great brand extensions there is of course a great product. Although clever marketing can persuade people to try a new product or service once, if the product or service does not deliver then repurchase and loyalty are unlikely to follow. There are two main performance issues to consider with extensions, as described by Professor Kevin Lane Keller (6). The first is having a 'point of parity' against the basic performance needs of the new segment or market. The second is a 'point of difference', which is the new benefit that the brand is bringing to the party.

Points of parity

Delivering against the basic needs in a new market is often overlooked in the rush for differentiation. Nivea waited many years before stretching from skin care into deodorants, as it had to find a way of delivering a skin-friendly product that would be really effective at odour protection. Without this point of parity, the extension was doomed to be a niche product, not an everyday one.

Points of difference

Assuming that a new product has the basics right, clearly it needs to offer a point of difference to have a decent chance of success. It is at this hurdle that many new launches fall, as they fail to bring anything new to the party. Timotei was a highly successful shampoo in Europe during the 1980s. Extending the gentle, mild, natural benefit into skin care seemed a logical move. However, the product experience lacked differentiation versus competitors such as Body Shop and Pure and Simple (7). The extension was a failure, despite heavy marketing support for advertising, promotion and point of sale.

There are several ways of delivering a point of difference, also discussed in Chapter 3:

- *Be unique*: Bertolli spreads deliver vitality and longevity as they are made with olive oil.
- *Overcommit*: Gillette has consistently overdelivered on the core benefit of close shaving by investing hundreds of millions of dollars to develop truly superior shavers.
- *Add a twist*: the round shape of Tetley's tea bags was more comfortable to use and fitted more easily into the bottom of the tea cup, helping increase share from 14 per cent in 1989 to 17 per cent in 1995.

The packaging dimension

Design is an incredibly rich source of differentiation, as it lives with the consumer throughout the life of the product, versus the more ephemeral nature of communication. The design

Improving product appeal

Enhancing product experience

Reinforcing brand imagery

Enhancing product delivery

Figure 6.6: Packaging as a differentiator.

Ariel packshot reproduced by permission of Procter & Gamble; Fruit Shoot packshot reproduced by permission of Britvic Soft Drinks Ltd; Gold Blend packshot reproduced by permission of Nestlé UK Ltd; Mentadent packshot reproduced by permission of Unilever HPC, NA.

dimension can help product delivery and improve product appeal, enhancing the product experience and reinforcing brand imagery (Figure 6.6).

Helping product delivery

Packaging can be used to help in delivering the product to offer extra benefits. In the USA Mentadent used innovative 'dual chamber' packaging to combine baking soda and peroxide to deliver a tooth-whitening toothpaste product. Previously, these two ingredients had to be combined by a dentist or specialist, owing to a potentially hazardous chemical reaction if the process was not done properly. This innovative product helped parent company Unilever double its share of the US toothpaste market in two years and go from being number five to number three in the market.

Improving product appeal

Packaging can make a huge difference to trial by enhancing the appearance of the product on the shelf. Sales of Ariel's new Liquitabs rocketed when they were repackaged in a transparent plastic box. This showed off the attractive little plastic pillows of green liquid, encouraging people to buy. An additional bonus is that the box can be reused around the kitchen as a handy container.

Enhancing the product experience

Packaging was a key factor that helped the Robinsons brand compete successfully in the UK children's drinks market. Most of the products on the market, such as Ribena, were sold in cardboard cartons and drunk with a straw. These tended to be messy and easy to spill. Robinsons children's offer first used the same generic packaging that was failing to meet the needs of consumers. Robinsons developed a highly attractive and impactful bottle for its new Fruit Shoot product, with a closure especially designed for children, based on the type of closure used on sports packs of water. Pulling the spout opens the flow of drink and pushing it back down seals the bottle, which made the drinking experience cleaner for parents. It also made the drink much more appealing for children, giving them a brand designed specifically for their needs, but took the pack codes of more adult drink consumption. The product was also differentiated, made with fruit puree plus added vitamins and a better taste. The distinctive pack helped the brand quadruple its share of the children's market over a two-year period.

Reinforcing brand image

Structural packaging can be a superb way of making your product look completely different and reinforcing the desired brand image. Nescafé has used packaging structure with huge success to reinforce the premium nature and taste values of its Gold Blend extension. This has been a key factor in differentiating it from retailers' own brands. As with the case of Gillette, Nescafé has not stopped at one pack innovation, starting out with a square cross-section pack but then following up with an even more distinctively shaped pack in the last couple of years.

Location, location, location

Distribution is a final aspect of delivering your promise that is perhaps more mundane than product and pack design, but is nonetheless just as important. 'Route to market' can be an incredibly strong weapon in the brand extension battle, and helps ensure that you deliver your promises by making the product easily available for consumers.

Coca-Cola is an obvious example of the power of distribution. Many experts say that the success of Coke is more to do with its supply chain than with any other element of the marketing mix. For example, Fanta has been able launch extensions such as Fruit Twist and Icy Lemon flavours in smaller outlets such as convenience stores, where Coke dominates the chiller cabinet. Competitor Tango has found this task a lot harder, as it does not have the same distribution muscle in this channel. When planning the launch of an extension, ensure that the distribution angle is not overlooked. Ask how Coke would go about launching the new product or service. How can you ensure that it was 'always within a hand's reach' of the consumer? Are there opportunities to piggy-back on other products and brands?

Key takeouts

1. Execution is just as important as strategy for a successful extension and not delivering against the promises made is a key reason for failure.
2. Getting execution wrong can also have a negative impact on other products in the range.
3. In contrast, brilliant products not only boost the chances of success, they also generate positive publicity for the brand.

Checklist 6: Delivery

	Yes	No
• Are you confident that you will fully deliver against the promises you are making in the extension concept?	☐	☐
• Are you working as hard on product and pack quality as you are on your brand strategy?	☐	☐
• Do you have at least one or two features that are newsworthy enough to get the extension talked about?	☐	☐
• Do you have a distribution strategy that creates competitive advantage for your extension?	☐	☐

 **Handover**

We have now completed the five key steps of the Brand Stretch programme, designed to help you boost the chances of extension success. We will finish off the book by addressing the important issue of brand architecture. This process will help you ensure that as your brand stretches you manage to promote extension platforms while also protecting the overall masterbrand equity. Such a strategy is crucial to ensure the best alignment of human and financial resources.

Step Six: Brand architecture

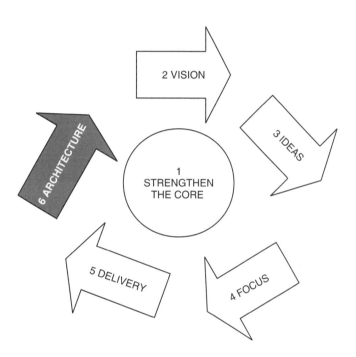

 Headlines

As a brand stretches it becomes a bigger challenge to manage and risks running off in too many directions. A multitude of messages confuses the consumer and dilutes the image of the masterbrand. It also leads to a loss of clarity on priorities within the company. The organizing system of 'brand architecture' helps solve these issues. It structures the brand's extended product range to aid navigation for the consumer and drive the optimum alignment of organizational resources.

The Sorcerer's Apprentice

As your brand's product range grows, you can end up like Mickey Mouse in *Fantasia*, when he played the Sorcerer's Apprentice. He turned one broom into two, then four, to help clean up. But before he knew it, he was overwhelmed with a multitude of brooms, each taking on a life of their own. A multiplying portfolio of extensions can land you with the same problem.

Company confusion

Without clear leadership, each product team will adapt the masterbrand positioning, identity and communication to maximize appeal to their target segment. If this is repeated across multiple extensions, the risk of brand dilution is obvious. In addition, investment decisions become much harder. How will you allocate the marketing spend? Which teams should get your star managers? Where should innovation efforts be focused? This confusion then gets transmitted to the rest of the business, leading to uncertainty and inefficiency. A critical area is the sales force, who often lose clarity on where to put their efforts. A common response is to focus on what is new and different, as this seems an easier sale than pushing the core products that have been around for years.

Consumer confusion

On average shoppers spend around 30 seconds in front of a fixture for a given category. Making their selection process more complicated by having a confusing product range means that your brand risks losing this battle for attention. Furthermore, if consumers receive too many mixed messages, the clarity of the masterbrand concept will be compromised.

Architecture for brands

When building a house, architecture guides the whole construction process, starting with the foundations, designing the layout of rooms and working right through to the look of the exterior. It plays a similar role in branding, only here we are organizing products and services into a manageable number of platforms (Figure 7.1). The objective of brand architecture can be summed up as follows:

> Structuring and organizing the brand's offer to aid consumer choice and maximize organizational efficiency.

Helping the consumer

Consumers can more quickly and easily *navigate the range* and find what they want. Rather than being faced with a plethora of products or services, these are grouped together based on similar benefits. In addition, architecture helps ensure that the *masterbrand concept* is clearly and powerfully communicated, so that consumers know where they stand with the brand.

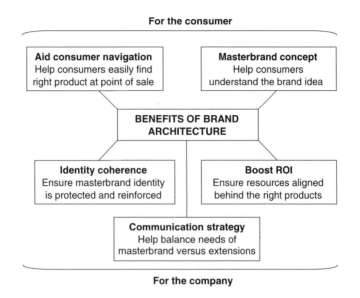

Figure 7.1: Brand architecture benefits.

Helping the organization

The most visible impact of brand architecture is on *naming and identity*. Here, the objective is to protect and reinforce the masterbrand identity (colours, logos, visual devices) and only change this when really necessary. However, architecture should also guide:

- *Resource alignment*: ensuring the best return on investment in both human and financial resources.
- *Communication strategy*: ensuring the right balance between the communication of the masterbrand and the extension concept.

Ideally, this process should of course be carried out before extension starts taking place. However, in reality it is often carried out after building work has begun! Even then, it should help not only organize the existing offer but also guide new innovation and extension. We will now look at the practical steps involved in designing a brand architecture, and the traps to avoid along the way.

Houses versus streets

The architecture approach will vary to a great extent on how stretched the brand is:

- *Product brands and tightly defined specialist brands* (e.g. Ariel/Tide, Pantene, Budweiser, Marlboro): you are developing the architecture for a single 'house'. There is a 'mono-platform' offer and the challenge is to structure the range of versions (different flavours and functionality) and formats (product and packs).

- *More stretched specialist brands and umbrella brands* (e.g. Nescafé, Dove, Colgate): the task is more to build a 'street' with several houses on it. There are multiple platforms to organize and the relationship between each of them and the masterbrand needs to be carefully considered.

We will now look at the specific challenges for each of these examples.

Mono-platform brands

Pantene is all about 'hair so healthy it shines'. The key architecture issues are developing the optimum range of versions/formats, finding the right consumer 'entry point' and maintaining coherence of the brand identity.

Value-added versioning

The role of versions is to deliver different functionality and/or flavours to meet the needs of different consumers or different usage occasions. (We looked at the use of market mapping to highlight opportunities for new versions back in Chapter 4.) Care should be taken to ensure that versions are meeting real consumer needs, and that these benefits are clearly communicated. In addition, a specific product or ingredient 'story' can help support each of these claims (Table 7.1).

For service brands the range of different offerings to organize is very large. The luxury business hotel chain Intercontinental tackled this by regrouping more than 50 different service offerings into four main areas, which are communicated to the consumer in advertising and in the hotel. These services are intended to help demonstrate the idea that Intercontinental really understands what senior business people need from a hotel, captured in the tagline 'We know what it takes'. For example, 'Around the clock' offers such services as the option to use the gym and pool at any time of the day and night. 'In an instant' includes super-fast check-in and the ability to get your local paper on the day it comes out, not a day later. This structure helps business travellers pick services relevant to them and builds understanding of the overall brand concept. For the company, it provides four areas on which to focus innovation and internal communication.

Formats that are fit for purpose

The second key dimension concerns the product formats offered. In the case of the Ariel/Tide laundry cleaning brand, the formats offered are 'big box' powders, tablets and liquids. Clarity

Table 7.1: Versioning summary for Pantene.

Versions ⇒	Classic Care = Anchor	Smooth and Sleek	Sheer Volume	Radiant Colour
	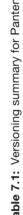			
Entry point = hair type/benefit	All hair types: simply clean, healthy-looking, shiny hair	Frizzy, fly-away hair: smooth away roughness, flyaways and frizz	Hair lacking body: 80% more volume from morning until night	Coloured, treated hair: preserve hair colour
Truth = specific product story	Pro-V formula	Smoothing Pro-V formula	Pro-V formula + amplifying structure builders	Pro-V formula + Gentle cleansers, damage-protection agents

Images reproduced by permission of Procter & Gamble.

Table 7.2: Format summary for a laundry cleaning brand.

	'Big box' powders	**Tablets**	**Liquids**
Fit for which purpose	Traditional format for older consumers wary of innovation, allowing dosing control	More convenient and modern format for busy people	More modern format for people concerned about clothes care and product aesthetics
Product format support	Simple, straightforward, no nonsense, big size impression	Compact, easy to dose, easy to transport and store	More in-use pleasure and care cues: translucent bottle, aquamarine colour, stronger fragrance
Price per wash index	100	150	125

is needed on the specific benefit each of these formats delivers that makes it fit for specific types of usage for defined consumer targets (Table 7.2).

Consumer entry point

A decision needs to be taken on whether formats or versions are to be the main 'entry point' for consumers. For example, Pantene uses versions, reflecting a belief that consumers are heavily influenced by their hair type when choosing a product, whether it be a shampoo, conditioner or hair spray. The Pantene.com website uses hair type versions as the main way to navigate the site and find the right product. In addition, communication has promoted the launch of new versions (Smooth & Sleek, Sheer Volume etc.) rather than merely selling the specific benefits of the different formats (shampoo, conditioner or styling product). This approach helps communicate the brand's expertise in haircare, by showing that it understands the needs of different hair types.

Although a main entry point may be selected, flexibility is needed to adapt to competitive threats and market trends. When the Dove brand launched a new shampoo in Europe, Pantene went back to communicating the specific benefits of the shampoo format to defend its position.

Avoiding duplication

The tendency is for brands to launch every version in every format, resulting in confusion and complexity. With just four extensions, a mono-product brand suddenly has a plethora of nine products (Figure 7.2). More discipline about the version/format matrix can simplify

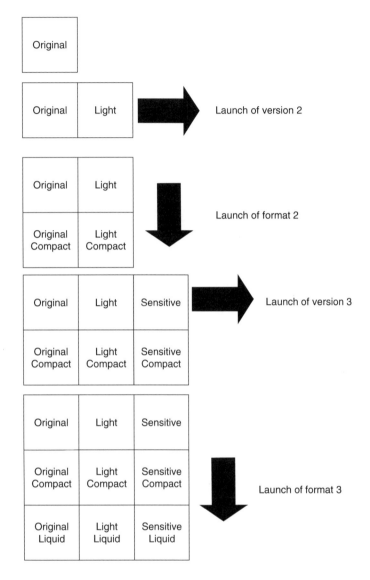

Figure 7.2: Four extensions = 9 × the complexity!

the offer, by only launching formats that are appropriate for each version (Table 7.3). For example, Pantene offers the basic shampoo and conditioner on all versions, but other more specialist products only on selected versions (e.g. root booster spray on the Sheer Volume version that gives more body and volume).

The bottom-line benefits of 'cleaning up' the versions and formats on a brand can be substantial, by clarifying the concept for consumers and the company. For example, one

Table 7.3: Versioning and format summary for Pantene.

Pantene packshot reproduced by permission of Procter & Gamble.

Versions ==>	Classic Care = Anchor	Smooth and Sleek	Sheer Volume	Radiant Colour
Entry point = hair type/benefit	All hair types: simply clean, healthy-looking, shiny hair	Frizzy, fly-away hair: smooth away roughness, flyaways and frizz	Hair lacking body: 80% more volume from morning until night	Coloured, treated hair: preserve hair colour
Truth = specific product story	Pro-V formula	Smoothing Pro-V formula	Pro-V formula + amplifying structure builders	Pro-V formula + Gentle cleansers, damage-protection agents
Shampoo	Yes	Yes	Yes	Yes
Conditioner	Yes	Yes	Yes	Yes
Hairspray	Yes	Yes	Yes	– (hair too fragile)
Styling gel	Yes	Yes	Yes: lifting gel	– (hair too fragile)
Styling mousse	Yes	Yes: controlling mouse	Yes: volumizing mousse	– (hair too fragile)
Smoothing cream	–	Yes: to help control fly-away hair	–	–
Root booster spray	–	–	Yes: to boost volume	–
Moisturising masque	–	–	–	Yes: for extra care

Version detail: Entry point, Truth

Standard formats: Shampoo, Conditioner, Hairspray, Styling gel, Styling mousse

Special formats: Smoothing cream, Root booster spray, Moisturising masque

Sheer Volume range

beer brand in eastern Europe cut the number of products in its range in half and actually saw sales *increase* by 50 per cent. In addition, by reducing complexity costs can be cut out of the business. One study showed that the cost *per item* of producing a mono-product range was between 25 and 45 per cent lower than that of a multi-product range (1).

Identity coherence

For a mono-platform brand, the consistency of the masterbrand identity should be maintained, with the role of design to help consumers find the right version for them. For example, the Persil brand in the UK portrays the core user of each version on pack while also respecting the masterbrand codes (logo, 'sun-burst' device). This helps navigation and also brings to life the brand's joyful, upbeat and optimistic personality (Figure 7.3). Remember that the way things look is just as important as what they are called. Consumers tend to use visual shorthand to navigate brands ('I like the green one, not the blue one') rather than knowing the exact descriptors ('I buy Persil Performance rather than Non-Bio').

Figure 7.3: Consistent masterbrand identity for a mono-platform brand.

Multi-platform brands

The architecture challenge is bigger when several platforms need to be managed, as the risks of fragmentation and masterbrand dilution are much higher. The temptation is to launch into naming and brand identity discussions straight away, but this should be avoided. A clear strategic framework should be developed to guide this and other decisions such as investment allocation.

Step one: How many platforms?

In this first step we need to develop the right number of platforms under which current and future products can be housed. This involves grouping together products that target similar consumer needs or occasions. Products within each platform will then share a similar look, feel, message and mix. Teams tend to overestimate the number of platforms that are necessary.

For example, the Lipton tea brand in the USA used to work with four different platforms: tea bags, iced tea, cold brew (home-made style) and Lipton Breeze (a carbonated soft drink). Different positionings had been developed for each platform, encouraging each team to develop its own marketing mix and resulting in unnecessary cost and complexity. Also, the masterbrand identity was diluted, with each platform having its own look and feel. On closer examination there was a large degree of consistency in the *content* of these platforms, even if the wording varied. It was agreed to treat tea as one single platform, with three different products (Figure 7.4) sharing a common identity and communication. In contrast, Breeze *was* a separate sub-branded platform that needed to stretch further in order to compete effectively with soft drinks like Coke.

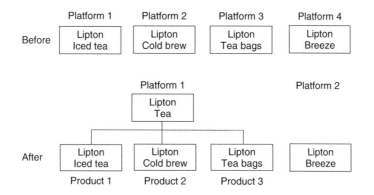

Figure 7.4: Platform picking.

Reducing the number of platforms can help you get a lot more bang for your buck, as shown by the example of Wrigley's chewing gum in the UK. Up until 2001 the brand was investing behind four different platforms, each with its own positioning, purchase brand and mix. Wrigley's Extra (fresh breath and confidence) and Wrigley's Airwaves (nose clearing) were big platforms that were growing well. However, despite major marketing support, both Wrigley's Orbit (oral care) and Wrigley's Ice White (teeth whitening) were small and declining (Table 7.4). The solution was for the Orbit dental care brand to 'adopt' the Ice White whitening product, creating a single oral health and beauty platform. This allowed the funds to be spent behind one big idea rather than two small ideas.

Step two: Family ties

The next step is to understand the relationship between each extension platform and the masterbrand. Key differences should be highlighted, along with a rationale for these changes (a tool for doing this will be discussed in the next step, along with the detailed questions to ask). Avoid the temptation to tweak and fiddle with every element of the masterbrand positioning. Rather, change fewer things but make a real difference to reflect the marketing challenge at hand. The degree of difference will then drive the naming and identity decisions at which we will look next.

Step three: Identity

With the right number of platforms in place, and the relationships between them and the masterbrand established, attention can turn to the visible manifestation of the brand architecture. The right naming and identity solution depends on the degree and type of

Table 7.4: Investing over too many platforms.

	1 Fresh breath and confidence: Extra	2 Nose clearing: Airwaves	3 Tooth protection: Orbit	4 Tooth whitening: Ice White
Retail sales £million	69	31	27	16
% change in sales (Year to July 01)	+16.5%	+29%	−3.4%	−14.7%
% Ad spend 2000 £million	4.4	5.7	3.3	3.9
% spend/sales	6%	18%	12%	24%

Combine into a single oral health & beauty platform

stretch from the masterbrand. We discussed this question in Chapter 5 when considering an individual extension; now we will consider the implications for the range as a whole.

Next door

When the stretch of the extension platform is small and mainly functional, coherence versus the masterbrand should be maintained. There may be a more specific target, benefit and supporting product truth. However, the values and personality remain the same. Brand identity execution between platforms should respect the masterbrand codes quite tightly. This approach can be seen in the stretch of Imperial Leather from soap into shower and bath products (Figure 7.5). Notice the use of descriptive names (e.g. Bathtime, Shower Gel) and the similar hierarchy of information and graphic design.

Up the street

In other cases, more stretch from the core may be needed to appeal to the target audience. This may involve emotional not just functional changes, with a slightly different personality. Sub-branding should only be used when really necessary, as significant investment is needed to communicate it properly; don't get kidded into thinking that a fancy name and new logo will do the job. Also, beware of sub-brands being managed as if they were 'grown-up' brands in their own right, with dedicated staffing and separate marketing support. This pushes them further away from the masterbrand than is really necessary.

Core product (soap)	Extension platform 1 (bathtime)	Extension platform 2 (shower gel)

Figure 7.5: Maintaining masterbrand coherence.

Figure 7.6: Two separate platforms that feel like new brands.

For a time in the 1990s this seemed to happen with Nescafé's super-premium exotic coffees. Advertising from this period shows how both Cap Colombie (Columbian blend) and Alta Rica (Arabica blend) received their own marketing support (Figure 7.6). Notice also a branding hierarchy on the pack that looks like a new brand (e.g. Alta Rica) with endorsement from Nescafé.

A better architecture has now been designed to treat these products as one single platform (Figure 7.7). The relationships between the core product, this platform and another key platform, Gold Blend, are summarized in Table 7.5. Notice how the values, rallying call and insight are consistent with the masterbrand. The platform has a slightly different target, and then delivers a specific twist on the brand promise of giving a 'coffee lift' to everyday life. This is supported by a specific benefit, truth and personality and a distinctive design, pack shape and colour. However, the platform still clearly feels like part of the same family and the naming hierarchy has been fine-tuned to clarify that the purchase brand is Nescafé. To push this change to its final conclusion, a range name would be used (e.g. 'Coffees of the World') along with simpler descriptive names for each version (e.g. 'Columbian blend' instead of Cap Colombie).

Different brand?

Warning signs should start to flash if an extension platform is so different from the masterbrand that the only link between them is a shared name; the extension platform is effectively a new brand in disguise. This is the worst of all worlds, as the extension is neither reinforcing the masterbrand nor having complete freedom to exploit the new positioning territory fully. In this case, one option is to bring the extension platform back in line with the masterbrand positioning, though this may compromise the ability of the extension to go after the new market opportunity and compete. The alternative is to separate the extension and manage it as a different brand, perhaps with some low-key endorsement from the original masterbrand.

For example, the Italian beer Peroni had a more premium, up-market sub-brand called Peroni Nastro Azzuro, targeted at young, urban people. Its positioning was almost the opposite from the core Peroni product, which was cheaper, more traditional and drunk by older people. In the end a decision was taken to unleash Nastro Azzuro and let it carve out its own positioning by removing the Peroni branding.

Step four: Product range by platform

Within each platform, the versioning and format offer needs to be designed, as discussed earlier in the section on mono-platform brands. An example of this for Imperial Leather's

Table 7.5: Relationship between extension platforms and masterbrand.

Platform	Nescafé Masterbrand/Original (Core product)	Nescafé Gold Blend (Extension platform 1)	Nescafé Exotic (Extension platform 2)
Positioning:			
– Market definition	• Hot drink products/services giving taste enjoyment and mood change (up or down)	• *Premium* hot drink products/services giving taste enjoyment and mood change (up or down)	• *Connoisseur* hot drink products/services giving taste enjoyment and mood change (up or down)
– Target	• People who care enough about coffee to choose one with a taste and aroma they really like	• People who care enough about coffee to choose one *that's a bit more special, even if it costs a bit more*	• People who care enough about coffee to choose one *that has specific origins and a more pronounced taste*
– Insight	*The taste and aroma of coffee provide not just physical pleasure but also emotional enhancement of the moment*	*The taste and aroma of coffee provide not just physical pleasure but also emotional enhancement of the moment*	*The taste and aroma of coffee provide not just physical pleasure but also emotional enhancement of the moment*
– Promise	• The coffee lift that picks me up during the hustle and bustle of everyday life	• The coffee lift that gives *coffee lovers a small moment of individual pleasure*	• The coffee lift that gives me *an enjoyable and exotic escape*
– Benefits	• The familiar taste and aroma you like: like a really good friend	• *Richer, fresher taste and aroma*	• *Deeper, more intense flavour and aroma*

– Truths	• Coffee-making expertise/experience • Original = UK's favourite coffee taste	• Coffee-making expertise/experience • *Real granules; distinctive jar shape*	• Coffee-making expertise/experience • *Distinctive, dark black jar; authentic, specific origins*
– Values	• Enjoying the moment; discernment	• Enjoying the moment; discernment	• Enjoying the moment; discernment
– Personality	• On my side; successful; popular	• *Exclusive; romantic; demanding*	• *Exotic; mysterious; deep*
– Rallying call	• FULL FLAVOURED LIFE	• FULL FLAVOURED LIFE	• FULL FLAVOURED LIFE
Image effect: **– Reinforces**	• –	• Individual enjoyment/pleasure	• Individual enjoyment/pleasure
– Adds	• –	• Premiumness, coffee quality	• Exoticism, discovery, authenticity
– Subtracts	• –	• –	• Less everyday
Stretch **– Functional**	• –	• Small	• Medium
– Emotional	• –	• Medium	• Medium
Branding Versions	• Descriptor • Normal, decaffeinated	• Sub-brand • Normal, decaffeinated. *Black Gold (richer taste)*	• Sub-brand • Normal only, *no decaffeinated*
Format	• One jar type, big/medium/small sizes	• One jar type, big/medium/small sizes	• One jar type, *medium/small sizes only*

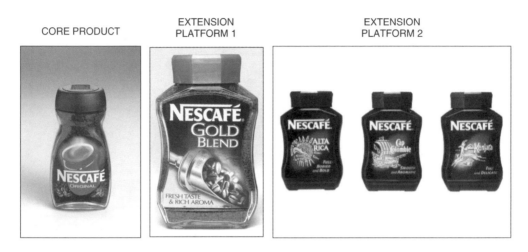

Figure 7.7: Different platforms for Nescafé.

Reproduced by permission of Nestlé UK Ltd.

Bathtime platform is shown in Table 7.6. See how in this case the brand decided to use formats rather than versions as the entry point. This is based on the insight that people choose the type of product format first, then select the fragrance they want.

Step five: The million-dollar questions

We saw in Chapter 5 the need to be ruthless in selecting the biggest extensions to launch, based on business and brand building potential. The same discipline is needed when deciding on ongoing launch support for different platforms. The tendency is to spread the marketing money too thinly, leading to fragmentation of human and financial resources. The following example looks at how Nescafé might have managed this process:

- *Cash builder = Original*: the original red jar of coffee might not be the sexiest part of the Nescafé brand, but it is by far the biggest, with retail sales of about $300 million in 2001 (2). Therefore, it has received a fair amount of dedicated marketing support, with a $45 million relaunch behind a more distinctive jar and new communication in 2002.
- *Hero = Gold Blend*: the most powerful vehicle to communicate the Nescafé brand vision and also a substantial profit contributor. It has sales of $150 million but is sold at a significant premium to Nescafé Original. This platform also gets its own campaign and major marketing support.
- *Niche products = Exotic*: these help reinforce the brand's coffee credentials and compete against ground coffee, but they are small in sales. We saw earlier how too much money had been spent on Cap Colombie and Alta Rica given their size. However, these funds

Table 7.6: Formats and versions for an extension platform.

IMPERIAL LEATHER MASTERBRAND		
Core product = soap	Extension platform 1 = bathtime	Extension platform 3 = shower

BATHTIME PLATFORM		
Formats =>	**Bubble Melts**	**Double Bubble**	**Bubbleburst Scentsations**
Entry point = usage experience	Skin-caring bubble bath	Rich, indulgent bubble bath	Sumptuous soft bubbles and fragrance hit
Truth = specific product story	Liquid bubbles contain gentle cleansers and concentrated moisturizers	Two liquids that combine: i) moisturizing milk extract, ii) fragrance and gentle cleanser	Spray into the running bath water and mousse releases bubbles and an amazing fragrance

Double Bubble versions		
Versions =>	**Unwind**	**Tranquillity**	**Replenish**
Specific benefit	Leave everything behind and relax	Zen-like relaxation	Refresh your body and mind
Ingredient story	Orange and Honey Milk	Green Tea and Avocado Milk	Mango and Peach Milk

have been reduced and they have to survive mainly on the 'halo' from the rest of the brand support.

- *Drain = Hot When You Want*: we saw in Chapter 6 how this product scored poorly on both business and brand vision building, because the product did not heat up the coffee properly. The sensible decision was taken to kill this product and go back to the drawing board.

Step six: Future focus

Brand architecture should not only help you put your existing house in order, it should also guide and inspire the development of new extensions. We will now look at an example of this with the story of Lego brand's rejuvenation.

Lego: Building blocks of a new future

Toy brand Lego was on the ropes in 2000, with losses of $130 million reflecting a collapse in sales. One of the key factors explaining the brand's problems was a lack of clarity in its architecture. Lego had stretched in many different directions, with no clear structure to explain the logic behind these moves. For example, Duplo targeted toddlers, Lego Scala tried to increase appeal to girls, and products with characters such as Harry Potter were also appearing (see Figure 7.8). To make matters worse, the company took an ego trip and tried to become a lifestyle brand, launching clothing lines, accessories and watches. As one article observed, 'Management is diluting the brand with a thousand extensions. This confuses children and their parents, many of whom grew up with Lego' (3). All this complexity also confused the company itself, with people inside the business no longer clear about the brand's purpose or direction.

Reconnecting with the roots

The first step in getting the brand back on track was to reconnect with Lego's roots and clarify the brand's promise and values. This work pinned down a promise of 'Encouraging self-expression by enabling children of all ages to bring endless ideas to life'. Importantly,

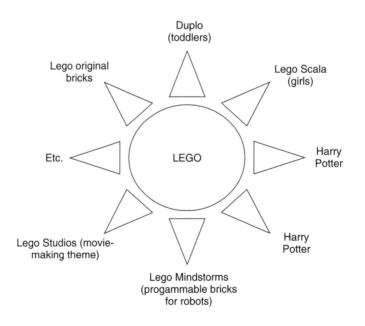

Figure 7.8: Too many directions – Lego in 2000.

this refocused the team on what was motivating and different about Lego: the fact that children built things themselves, and were able to produce infinite results. The new vision was summed up with the rallying call of 'Play on', which worked well as a consumer message but also as a call to action for people in the business. In addition it reconnected powerfully with the brand's heritage: the name Lego is a contraction of a Danish phrase meaning 'play well'.

New doors into the brand

The next step for the brand was summed up well by Francesco Ciccolella, the senior vice-president of global branding:

> We needed to put some order into our house. We knew there were some major challenges to face – the expression of the brand was not coherent enough, the brand architecture was too complicated (4).

The solution was to structure the range based on four platforms, or portals as the brand calls them (Table 7.7). Each of these was based on a different type of interactive play, helping parents more easily find the right product for their child's needs and interests. For example, Lego Next provides a more challenging and grown-up form of construction than simply sticking bricks together. Lego Mindstorms is one of the star products in this platform, allowing children to build robots but also program them to act as they wish. Anchoring each platform on a clear play idea also helped reinforce communication of the brand promise.

The new architecture also improved organizational efficiency. Discipline was applied in managing products that did not fit into any of the four portals. Lego branding on these extensions was reduced to a low-key endorsement and will only be changed if the offer can

Table 7.7: New Lego architecture.

Platform =>	Lego Explore	Lego Stories and Action	Lego Make and Create	Lego Next
Type of product	Different coloured and shaped Lego bricks to help children learn and grow while having fun	Construction with emphasis on bringing to life different character universes	More challenging and complex construction, with maximum flexibility of outcome	High-tech, programmable creation kits
Core age group	0–5	4–8	7–10	10+
Examples of versions	Explore being me Explore together Explore logic	Harry Potter Bionicles Star Wars	Lego Technic Construction designer kits	Lego Mindstorms robots Lego Spybotics

be redesigned to fit better with the brand promise. In addition, innovation efforts on new extensions are only funded if they help build one of the portals.

Back on track

The early signs are that the brand is back on track for growth, with 2001 seeing a profit of $70 million and 14 per cent revenue growth in the all-important US market. One key move that should help the new strategy have a positive impact on the business is the serious investment in explaining the new promise and architecture to people inside the business via the Lego Brand School, which has been visited by more than 1000 staff. As we saw earlier, architecture is not just about brand identity, it is about clarifying where the brand's investment and innovation efforts should be focused.

> ### Lego summary
>
> 1. An unclear architecture leads to confusion for consumers and the company.
> 2. Extension platforms make finding the right product at point of sale much easier.
> 3. Done well, architecture can also help communicate the brand concept.

With a clear idea of the brand platforms, a key task is to figure out how to communicate these to the consumer in advertising and other media.

When the rubber hits the road

Balancing the conflicting needs of communicating product-specific messages and building a master brand is a real headache from which most major companies are suffering. To help you choose the right approach you must be crystal clear on your objectives. The five main strategies we will look at go from the most masterbrand focused through to the most product focused (Figure 7.9): brand campaign episode, brand backbone, brand property, family feel and stand-alone (Figure 7.10). As with all marketing, there is no 'right' or 'wrong' solution, only the one that you feel is best for your particular situation.

Option one: Brand campaign episodes (Dove)

This approach works well for mono-platform brands or those with several platforms that are close together. A single masterbrand campaign idea and execution is used to support each extension that is advertised. For example, Dove uses real women sharing their experiences and how they have been pleasantly surprised by the brand's performance. The major advantages of this route are the savings in creative development and execution plus the consistency of

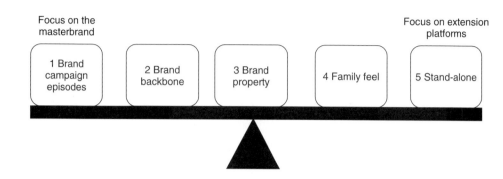

Figure 7.9: The brand balancing act.

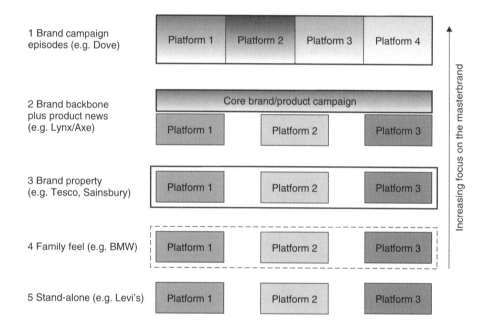

Figure 7.10: Communication strategies.

masterbrand message. The challenge is getting across the product-specific message, as the masterbrand campaign idea is dominant. Also, adapting the personality and tone of voice for different targets is difficult.

Option two: Brand backbone (Axe/Lynx)

This approach is right for teams who are committed to building a strong masterbrand and core product, but who also need to launch a steady stream of new innovations. It has been used successfully by Axe/Lynx body spray for young men to build a 37 per cent share of UK male deodorants and 80 per cent penetration of boys 15–19 (5). A humorous, tongue-in-cheek core campaign dramatizes the 'Lynx effect' that helps you smell great, feel confident and so get the girl. This brand backbone campaign reinforces and strengthens the masterbrand positioning, but also builds sales of the core product range. Importantly, it is not 'brand anthem' communication that promotes a philosophy without any direct link to a product.

Additional support is used to promote the launch of new extensions. This is a key part of keeping the brand fresh and interesting for a fickle target, with the idea that each new generation feels it has its own Lynx, in the same way that it would have its favourite Madonna song. These extensions are developed and launched in the same way as a fine fragrance. The team uses an understanding of contemporary cultural cues and codes to develop a name, concept and fragrance. For example, the launch of Phoenix came immediately after the fall of the Berlin Wall, tapping into the new optimism without directly referencing the theme. Each new extension is also managed as an event to create news value and excitement. Voodoo was one of the brand's most successful launches, creating hype through eclipse parties, dance events and concerts.

Option three: Brand property (Walkers)

This approach is one of the most popular for stretched brands, as it strikes a balance between building the masterbrand and promoting extension platforms. It uses a brand property such as a celebrity or character to provide consistency and the development of the masterbrand personality. The Walkers brand of potato chip (Lay's in the USA) has used a campaign featuring the ex-England soccer captain Gary Linneker for many years, with a total of 37 executions to date! The campaign is based on the idea that the products are so irresistible that you would do anything to get them. The first execution, called 'No more Mr Nice Guy', showed Gary, famous for fair play, getting his hands on some Walkers by stealing a packet off a young fan. Over the years, this campaign has been used to promote a series of range extensions, including low fat, Salt and Shake and Sensations. Another good example of this approach is the use of Jamie Oliver by Sainsbury's, the UK retailer. Here, a common endline, 'Making life taste better', is used to help communicate a consistent masterbrand promise.

The challenge, especially as the campaign becomes more established, is to achieve stand-out for the extension. The risk is that consumers see the brand but fail to remember which product is being featured. The UK supermarket Tesco has moved to a stand-alone campaign for its personal finance offer after initially promoting it as part of its long-running 'Every little helps' campaign starring Prunella Scales as Dotty.

Option four: Family feel (BMW)

This strategy starts to move the weight of communication much more towards the extension platform. It works well when the brand has a flow of product innovation to introduce and wants to give each extension platform more of a distinctive personality. The family feel is mainly maintained via executional devices such as logos, slogans and tone of voice.

BMW is a good example of a brand using this approach. Communication of each new car line does have a product-specific message and campaign. At the same time, it is often quite clear that you are seeing communication for BMW rather than another car marque. Some of the key brand properties that help create a family feel are as follows:

- *Slogan*: every BMW car is promoted as 'the ultimate driving machine' in its category. This slogan encapsulates the brand promise in an extremely powerful and memorable way.
- *Style and tone*: BMW develops different commercials for each new extension. However, there is a consistent style and tone to the brand's communication that makes it feel BMW-like. The communication is consistently minimalist, emphasizes product performance, and has a high quality of art direction and photography.
- *Identity execution*: strong brands have a consistent way of executing their visual identity, made up of logos and other visual devices. For example, the BMW logo and strapline appear in the same place across different press adverts.

Option five: Stand-alone (Levi's)

At the other end of the support spectrum is the stand-alone approach, where the extension platform has a starring role. The message is focused on what is specific to the new product or service and each piece of communication takes on a different tone, style and personality. This approach is most appropriate for sub-branded platforms where the stretch from the core product is both functional and emotional. However, it should really be used as a last resort, as the cost is high, for both commercial production and media. Many of the cost benefits of extending an existing brand are lost.

Levi's uses stand-alone communication for its new sub-branded product lines. The successful launch of the twisted jean, Levi's Engineered, was a key part of reversing the downward decline that the brand had suffered in the mid to late 1990s. This product needed to dramatize a newer, edgier face of Levi's in order to win back young people, who influence fashion trends. The initial advertising showed young people with body parts that could also twist and achieved the stand-out the brand was looking for. The brand is trying to follow the success of twisted with another new sub-brand called Type A. Again, this has been launched with a new stand-alone campaign with the idea of a 'brand new breed'.

To end the book we will now look at the growth story of the Comfort brand, in order to tie together the key ideas in this and previous chapters.

Comfort: Designing a turnaround

In the early 1990s, Comfort fabric softener (Snuggle in the USA) was in decent health although sales were stable. The core blue product had a strong image, but the brand's range lacked differentiation versus key competitor Lenor, having several simple versions with basic fragrances (e.g. Spring fresh). A new masterbrand positioning and architecture helped relaunch the brand and accelerate growth. By the year 2004 it is estimated that the brand will have doubled in size.

A new promise

The team members started by applying the principles of brand vision. They redefined the market as not just fabric softener, but as wearing, washing, drying, ironing and storing clothes. A valuable insight nugget was uncovered during this process: clothes are like people, in that looking after them with care makes them look, feel and smell much better. This led to a brand promise along the lines of 'personal care for clothes', which was still rooted in the brand's benefit of caring for clothes, but put more emphasis on the personal pleasure in the process (Figure 7.11 has my go at the positioning). The idea was to borrow some of the codes from health and beauty care brands to develop a more motivating and distinctive brand mix and more emotional appeal versus Lenor.

From promise to platforms

Three key extension platforms were developed and new innovations launched under each platform to renew and reinforce them (Figure 7.12). Stretch in each case was mainly functional, so coherence with the masterbrand identity has been maintained and descriptive names used.

Hedonistic care

This platform was created using the fine fragrance category as a source of inspiration. It built on an understanding that the pleasant smell of a fabric softener was a key reason for purchase. The brand boldly broke out of conventional, dull versioning. Working with fragrance experts, the team identified key trends and developed new variants against these. The first new launch was Mandarin and Green Tea. In addition to a distinctive name, colour

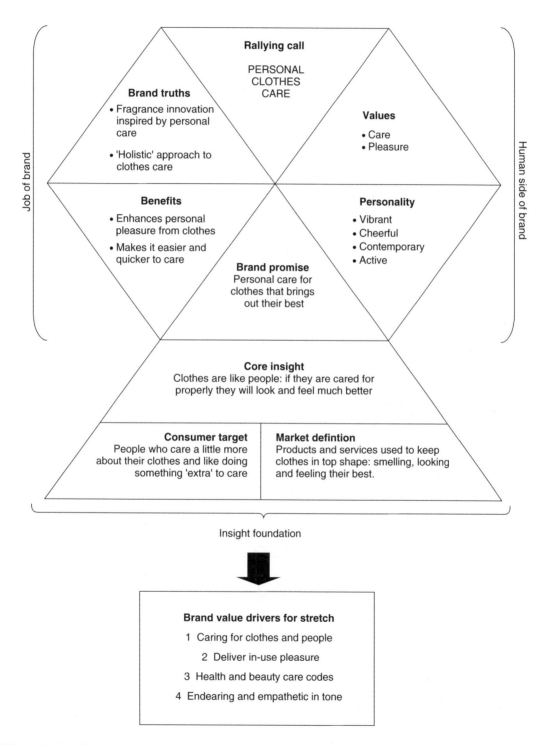

Figure 7.11: Comfort's masterbrand vision (author's own).

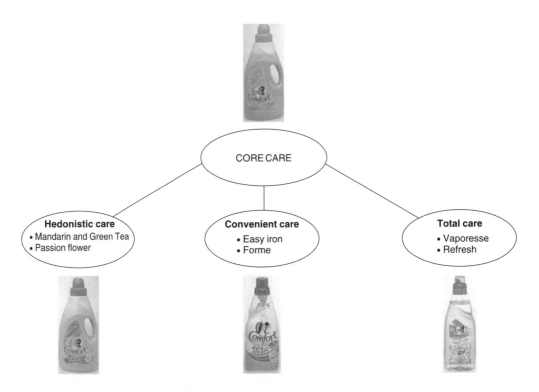

Figure 7.12: Comfort brand architecture.

was used to bring to life the concept and create impact on shelf. This product platform helped attract new users to the Comfort brand and also helped in the 'personal care for clothes' repositioning. The positioning for this platform 'dialled up' the pleasure aspect of the masterbrand, emphasizing the vibrant and cheerful side of Comfort's personality. Notice how the core insight, promise, values and essence stay the same, however. Further launches have included Passion Flower and Ylang Ylang and Lily and Riceflower. Importantly, as new extensions have been added, the weakest one in the existing range has been culled to avoid complexity.

Functional care

Looking at the clothes care process in a broader way showed that one of the biggest hassles in clothes care was ironing. This led to the development of a product called Easy Iron, which softens clothes but also makes them easier to iron afterwards. More recently, the brand has launched a second product under this platform called Comfort Forme, which helps clothes keep their shape better. In this platform the convenience aspects of the brand are emphasized. Again, the core elements of the masterbrand positioning remain the same.

Total care

From the same work on the wash and wear cycle, the team identified an opportunity to stretch beyond the washing machine. Comfort Vaporesse was a fragranced ironing water that helped make ironing easier and also made the clothes smell nicer. The great benefit of this extension was that is was almost 100 per cent incremental business with no cannibalization of existing products. This extension has added almost 10 per cent incremental business to the brand. It has the advantage of tapping into an existing habit and one that is a regular task (Table 7.8) for a go at the architecture.

From platforms to promotion

Comfort needed to promote a series of new innovations under each of the platforms while still establishing the big masterbrand idea of personal care for clothes. This led to the use of the brand property approach that we saw earlier, which strikes a good balance between these two needs. The masterbrand promise was brought to life in advertising by Darren and Lisa, the cloth puppets, who use the product on themselves like a moisturizer! This communication was truly disruptive versus the category codes of happy families, smiling children and piles of fresh laundry. It was also flexible enough to work in communicating messages for the functional and hedonistic care platforms (Figure 7.13). These two platforms were used to deliver a 'left–right' punch, by focusing on two complementary parts of the brand proposition.

Comfort is now a strong and healthy brand, having enjoyed growth of about 10 per cent for several years in a row. The core blue product is still at the heart of the brand, representing about a third of fabric softener sales. The hedonistic and functional platforms represent a further third each. The same strategy and mix has now been rolled out across Europe, but launched under local brand names (e.g. Cajoline in France, Robijn in the Netherlands).

> **Comfort summary**
>
> 1. Develop a broad market definition.
> 2. Use this to inspire a big master-brand idea.
> 3. Build platforms under which multiple products can be launched.

Table 7.8: Relationship between extension platforms and masterbrand (author's own version).

Platform	Masterbrand/Core product	Hedonistic care	Functional care
Positioning:			
– Market definition	• Products/services used to keep clothes smelling, looking and feeling their best	• Products/services used to keep clothes *smelling*, looking and feeling their best	• Products/services used to *conveniently* keep clothes smelling, looking and feeling their best
– Target	• People who care more about their clothes and so like to do a little 'extra' *for their family* when looking after them	• People who care more about their clothes and so like to do a little 'extra' *for themselves* when looking after them	• People who care more about their clothes and like to do a little 'extra' when looking after them but *are often too busy*
– Insight	*Clothes are like people: if they are cared for properly they will look and feel much better and give you more pleasure*	*Clothes are like people: if they are cared for properly they will look and feel much better and give you more pleasure*	*Clothes are like people: if they are cared for properly they will look and feel much better and give you more pleasure*
– Promise	• Personal care for clothes that brings out their best	• Personal care for clothes that brings out their best	• Personal care for clothes that brings out their best
– Benefits	• Enhances personal pleasure from clothes	• *Enhances personal pleasure from clothes*	• Enhances personal pleasure from clothes
	• Makes it easier/quicker to care	• Makes it easier/quicker to care	• *Makes it easier/quicker to care*
– Truths	• Innovation inspired by the world of health and beauty care and a 'holistic' approach to clothes care	• Innovation inspired by *the world of health and beauty care and a 'holistic' approach to clothes care*	• Innovation inspired by the world of health and beauty care and a 'holistic' approach to clothes care

– Values	• Care; pleasure	• Care; pleasure	• Care; pleasure
– Personality	• Vibrant; cheerful; active	• Vibrant; cheerful; active	• Vibrant; cheerful; *active*
– Rallying call	• PERSONAL CLOTHES CARE	• PERSONAL CLOTHES CARE	• PERSONAL CLOTHES CARE
Image effect:			
– Reinforces	• –	• Clothes care emotion	• Clothes care function
– Adds	• –	• Dials up fragrance/personal pleasure	• Dials up convenience
– Subtracts	• –	• Less about love of the family	• Risks lacking emotion, aspiration
Stretch			
– Functional	• –	• Small	• Small
– Emotional	• –	• Small	• Small
Branding	• Descriptor	• Products with descriptors	• Products with descriptors
Versions	• Original blue, pure	• Passion Flower & Ylang Ylang, Lily & Riceflower	• Easy iron, Forme
Format	• Normal/big, concentrated/small	• Normal/big, concentrated/small	• Concentrated/small

| Hedonistic care | Functional care |

Figure 7.13: Comfort platforms brought to life with a brand property-based campaign.

Reproduced by permission of Lever Fabergé. Fine Fragrance advert photography by Ray Massey – represented by Horton-Stephens.

Let's go round again

The Comfort story should hopefully tie together the key building blocks of the Brand Stretch workout. As a reminder, the key issues we have tried to address and the suggested solutions are summarized again in Table 7.9.

Table 7.9: Recap of brand ego trip problems and solutions.

Workout	Problem	Solution
1 Strengthen the core	Neglecting the core brand/product range	Protect and grow the core
2 Vision	Forgetting what made you famous in the first place	Clear vision to ensure extensions have added value
3 Ideas	Extensions are company not market driven	Use market and consumer insight as a catalyst for ideas
4 Focus	Scatter-gun stretching leads to dwarf extensions	Fewer, bigger ideas that build brand *and* business
5 Delivery	Execution fails to deliver against promises	Excellence in execution as a key source of differentiation
6 Brand architecture	Confusing range for both consumer and company	Structure that aids consumer choice and company efficiency

Key takeouts

1. Brand architecture helps structure and organize the product range to maximize efficiency for the company and ease consumer choice.
2. Product platforms should group products together, help stimulate innovation and show how each one helps build the masterbrand vision.
3. Where possible, strategic and executional consistency with the masterbrand should be maintained, with changes made only when the degree of stretch is substantial.

Checklist 7: Brand architecture

	Yes	No
• Do you have a series of extension platforms, each anchored on a consumer target, need or occasion?	☐	☐
• Do these extension platforms help build the masterbrand promise, rather than merely telling their own story?	☐	☐
• Is the brand architecture driving alignment of human and financial resources, and not just brand identity?	☐	☐
• Have you carefully considered the communication strategy options and got the one that best meets your brand and business goals?	☐	☐

 **Handover**

We have come to the end of the Brand Stretch workout. I hope that you have taken away a few practical pointers that will help you raise your chances of success and make your project one of the minority that survives and succeeds! Please do share with me stories of extension success *and* failure, as well as your points of view, as there is still a whole lot more to learn about the area of brand stretch. (Contact me at david@thebrandgym.com.)

Masterbrand positioning tips and tricks

Appendix 1: Positioning tips and tricks.

		Inspires and Guides	Tips and Tricks	Bad examples	Good examples
Insight foundation	Market definition	Full view of real competition, opportunities for stretch	Who wins when we lose? Use benefits not just product terms	Videotapes (Blockbuster)	Rentable home entertainment (Blockbuster)
	Positioning target	Empathy with the core consumer, understand their life	Capture attitudes, values, colour	AB women aged 25–45 (Knorr)	Food enthusiasts who enjoy good food but are pressed for time (Knorr)
	Core insight	Open the door to an opportunity to improve everyday life	Describe a human truth *and* how this opens a door for the brand; add colour and emotion	Parents worry about nappy rash (Pampers old)	Babies with healthy skin are happier and so more able to play, learn and develop (Pampers new)
	Brand truths (1–2)	Development of product features and attributes	Be specific and concrete	Good service (Blockbuster)	Blockbuster promise: 'Get the film you want or hire it for free next time'
Job of brand	Benefits (1–2)	Product development, communication emphasis	Specific reasons for purchase, not reasons to believe	Pro-vitamin B5; doesn't dry hair (Pantene)	Hair so healthy it shines (Pantene)
Human side	Values (1–2)	Issues to campaign on, brand behaviour with customers	Make them provocative and polarizing	Quality; teamwork (Pret a Manger)	Setting the bar high; one for all, all for one (Pret a Manger)
	Personality (2–3)	Guide tone, feel and style of communication and front-line staff	Make them colourful not bland	Reliable; honest; friendly (Clearasil)	Solid as a rock; straight as an arrow; best mate (Clearasil)

(continued overleaf)

Appendix 1: (*continued*)

		Inspires and Guides	Tips and Tricks	Bad examples	Good examples
Rallying calls	Promise (15–20 words)	Key idea for communication and innovation	Focused on what it is and why it's better; inject colour, emotion and edge	Affordable short-break holiday offering best combination of activities for all the family (DLP)	Magical place where everyone can live out adventures they have dreamt of (DLP)
	Rallying call/essence (2–4 words)	Shorthand summary that in spires and mobilizes the team	Capture emotion not just function, inspire future growth	Best shave (Gillette); male attractiveness (Axe)	Ultimate performance (Gillette); Pulling power (Axe)

Example masterbrand positioning tool

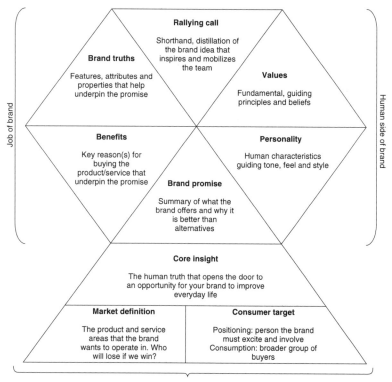

Rallying call

Shorthand, distillation of the brand idea that inspires and mobilizes the team

Brand truths

Features, attributes and properties that help underpin the promise

Values

Fundamental, guiding principles and beliefs

Benefits

Key reason(s) for buying the product/service that underpin the promise

Personality

Human characteristics guiding tone, feel and style

Brand promise

Summary of what the brand offers and why it is better than alternatives

Core insight

The human truth that opens the door to an opportunity for your brand to improve everyday life

Market definition

The product and service areas that the brand wants to operate in. Who will lose if we win?

Consumer target

Positioning: person the brand must excite and involve
Consumption: broader group of buyers

Job of brand

Human side of brand

Insight foundation

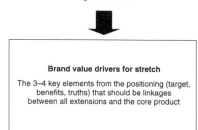

Brand value drivers for stretch

The 3–4 key elements from the positioning (target, benefits, truths) that should be linkages between all extensions and the core product

Masterbrand positioning tool template

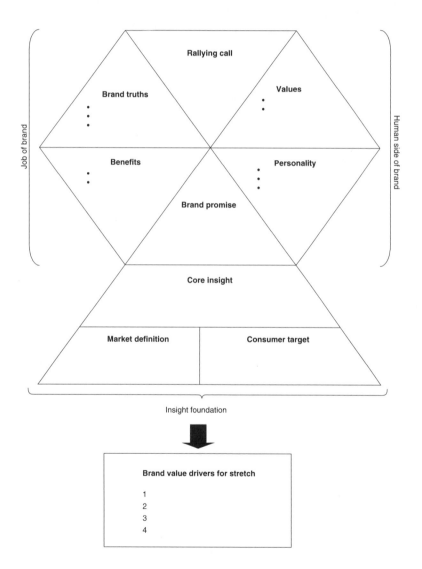

References

Preface

1 'A healthy gamble: How did A.G. Lafley turn Procter & Gamble's old brands into hot items?', *Time.com*, 16 September 2002.

Chapter 1

1 Kapferer, J.N. (1998) *Strategic Brand Management*, Kogan Page.
2 *Ibid.*
3 Ries, A. (1997) *Focus: The Future of Your Company Depends on It*, HarperCollins.
4 *HPI*, April 2002.
5 'Fool's gold for marketers', *Brand Strategy*, February 2003, 20–22.
6 Haig, M. (2003) *Brand Failures: The Truth about the 100 Biggest Branding Mistakes of all Time*, Kogan Page.

Chapter 2

1 Reddy, S.K., Holak, S.L. and Bhat, S. (1994) 'To extend or not extend: Success determinants of line extensions', *International Journal of Marketing Research*, Vol. 31, May, 243–62.
2 'Sports drinks step up the pace', *Marketing,* 13 March 2003, 15.
3 John, P.R. and Loken, B. (1998) 'The negative impact of extensions: Can the flagship be diluted?', *Journal of Marketing*, Vol. 62, January, 19–32.
4 'Smirnoff's cool extension', *Brand Strategy*, February 2003, 23.
5 Trout, J. (2002) *Big Brands, Big Trouble: Lessons Learned the Hard Way*, John Wiley & Sons Inc.
6 Haig, M. (2003) *Brand Failures: The Truth about the 100 Biggest Branding Mistakes of all Time*, Kogan Page.
7 'Biggest brands', *Marketing*, 15 August 2002, 20–27.
8 'Make or break overhaul for Tango', *Marketing Week*, 27 February 2003, 5.

Chapter 3

1 Taylor, D. (2002) *The Brand Gym: A Practical Workout for Boosting Brand and Business*, John Wiley & Sons.

2 Rangaswammy, A., Burke, R.R. and Olivia, T.A. (1993) 'Brand equity and the extendability of brand names', *International Journal of Research in Marketing*, Vol. 10, No. 1, 61–75.

3 Keller, K.L. (1998) *Strategic Brand Management: Building, Measuring and Managing Brand Equity*, Prentice Hall.

4 'Elastic brands', *Sunday Times*, 3 November 1996, 7.

5 'Retailers make a new financial play', *Marketing Week*, 30 January 2003, 19–20.

Chapter 4

1 www.thetimes100.co.uk.

2 'When brands bounce back', *Marketing,* 15 February 2001, 26–7.

3 The Marketing Society Awards 2002, Customer Insight winning case.

4 'FMCG innovator', *Marketing*, 23 January 2003, 23.

5 The Marketing Society Awards 2002, New Brand winning case.

6 'A breath of minty fresh air', *Brandweek.com,* 2 January 2003.

7 Haig, M. (2003) *Brand Failures: The Truth about the 100 Biggest Branding Mistakes of all Time*, Kogan Page.

8 'A healthy gamble: How did A.G. Lafley turn Procter & Gamble's old brands into hot items?', *Time.com*, 16 September 2002.

9 The Marketing Society Awards 2003, New Brand winning case.

10 Shultz, H. and Yang, D.J. (1997) *Pour Your Heart into It: How Starbucks Built a Company One Cup at a Time*, Hyperion.

11 'The perfect paradox of star brands', *Harvard Business Review*, October 2001, 116–23.

Chapter 5

1 'Brand MOT: Camelot', *Brand Strategy*, January 2003, 8.

2 Ries, A. (1997) *Focus: The Future of Your Company Depends on It*, HarperCollins.

3 Knobil, M. (editor-in-chief) (2001) *Superbrands,* Superbrands Ltd.

4 'Too cool for Chrysler?', *Wall Street Journal*, 21–22 July 2000, 25.

5 Keller, K.L. (1998) *Strategic Brand Management: Building, Measuring and Managing Brand Equity*, Prentice Hall.

6 Sood, S., Kirmain, A. and Brudegs, S. (1999) 'The ownership effect in consumer responses to brand line stretches', *Journal of Marketing*, Vol. 63, No. 1, January, 88–101.

7 'Easy does it – but not with everything', *Sunday Times,* 27 April 2003, 8.

8 '100 years on the road', *Marketing,* 8 May 2003, 24–5.

Chapter 6

1 'Nescafé discards self-heating cans', *Marketing*, 15 August 2002, 1.

2 Keller, K.L. (1998) *Strategic Brand Management: Building, Measuring and Managing Brand Equity*, Prentice Hall.

3 'Persil Power proved to have a bit too much zap', *Brand Strategy*, March 2003, 7.

4 'The ultimate creativity machine: How BMW turns art into profit', *Harvard Business Review*, January 2001, 47–55.
5 CNETnews.com, 24 October 2002.
6 Keller, K.L. (1998) *Strategic Brand Management: Building, Measuring and Managing Brand Equity*, Prentice Hall.
7 Lury, G. (1998) *Brandwatching*, Blackhall Publishing.

Chapter 7

1 Various authors (1999) *Harvard Business Review on Brand Management,* Harvard Business School Press.
2 'Grinding profits from beans', *Brand Strategy,* December 2002, 18–21.
3 'A brick too far', *Marketing Week,* 15 March 2001, 26–9.
4 'Building a brand out of bricks', *Brand Strategy,* April 2003, 16–19.
5 The Marketing Society Awards 2003, Marketing Achievement winning case.

Index